THE GOLDEN RULE

For Empowering Professional Relationships

Ignatius Fernandez

THE GOLDEN RULE

For Empowering Professional Relationships

Ignatius Fernandez

Wolf Creek Press
Bandon, OR USA
2014

The Golden Rule
For Empowering Professional Relationships

By Ignatius Fernandez

Wolf Creek Press
Bandon, OR USA

All rights reserved. No part of this book may be reproduced or transmitted in any form or by any means, electronic or mechanical, including photocopying, recording or by any information storage and retrieval system, without written permission from the author, except for the inclusion of brief quotations in a review.

The Golden Rule: For Empowering Professional Relationships
Ignatius Fernandez - 1st ed.
Cover design and back cover text by Konrad Fernandez.
Copyright © 2014 by Ignatius Fernandez

Printed and bound in the United States of America
First printing 2014

ISBN-13: 978-1495371752
ISBN-10: 1495371751

This book is dedicated to my students who responded positively to thoughts I shared with them on professional behavior and Jesus' teachings.

About the Author

Ignatius Fernandez, Senior Management Professional, Professor, Corporate Trainer and author, has brought to this book his hard-won experience in managing, teaching, training and counseling people of different age groups and backgrounds.

Other books by Ignatius Fernandez

- My Family – The Next Best Thing that Happened to Me
- Relationship Management – The Master's Way
- Through The Eye of a Needle – Transforming Relationships
- Life Lessons – A Christian Sharing
- The Heart Has Its Reasons - Looking Back, Looking Ahead

The Golden Rule

Contents

About the Author	i
Foreword	v
Chapter 01 - The 360 Degree Appraisal	1
Chapter 02 - The Relationship Model	17
Chapter 03 - The Source – The Gospels	37
Chapter 04 - The Age and Times	51
Chapter 05 - The Fully Human Professional	69
Chapter 06 - Relationship with the Team	107
Chapter 07 - Jesus and Professionals	127
Chapter 08 - Appraising Relationships	141
Chapter 09 - The People Person	171
Chapter 10 - The Perceptions of the Model	183
Chapter 11 - Sink or Sail Together	189

Chapter 12 - The Need to Change   201

Chapter 13 - The Change Agent   225

Chapter 14 - The Communicator   243

Chapter 15 - Leadership and Change   257

Chapter 16 - The Combination is Synergetic   269

Chapter 17 - Empowering Professional Relationships 285

Chapter 18 - Adopting New Standards   305

References   325

Foreword

The life and times of Jesus Christ have been analyzed from many perspectives, but never before so comprehensively from that of the corporate world and professional relationships, as in *The Golden Rule for Empowering Professional Relationships*.

Ignatius Fernandez has produced a scholarly and absorbing analysis of how Jesus Christ's behavior sets an example, not just for our personal lives, but also for our professional conduct, and gives a compelling and rigorous account of how Jesus was in fact the definitive leader in every respect.

Set within the context of a modern India boardroom, Ignatius Fernandez describes, from a practical, non-aligned standpoint, how the time-honored texts of Christianity reveal just how effectively Jesus conducted the business of his Mission, and serve as a comprehensive manual for modern corporate practices.

The Golden Rule

From skilful deployment of the spectrum of leadership styles, only recently re-discovered and re-articulated in the best-sellers of today's business gurus, through to effective communications, marketing, teamwork, recruitment, delegation, performance management, and work-life balance, *The Golden Rule* systematically reveals, with meticulous reference to the actual events recorded in the Gospels, just how far Jesus Christ set the standards in these management fields, and how much there is to learn from his example.

This unique insight makes a novel and seminal contribution to our understanding both of business management, and of the politics of Jesus Christ's own times, in which the parallels to our modern corporate world are only too recognizable.

The conclusion of the piece, delivered at the climax of a cleverly crafted plot which keeps the pages turning, is at once a revelation and a time-honored truth. The Golden Rule is a maxim to which many pay lip service, while failing to understand its immensely powerful potential for our personal and professional lives. It is at once a lesson and a guide for our daily existence, as well as a sure means of delivering the win-win scenarios which are the true definition of business success.

Paul Sellers

Director, South India, British Council, London.

The Golden Rule

Chapter 1

The 360 Degree Appraisal

- *"Nothing is as easy as it looks.*
- *Everything takes longer than you think.*
- *If anything can go wrong, it will."*

   Murphy's Law

Alex Thomas, Vice President, Marketing, of Mount Pharmaceuticals, Chennai, India, was busy during the week end, not with personal chores, but with professional duties that had a bearing on his career. He worked on his Annual Appraisal Form and gave it finishing touches after repeatedly going over figures from notes he carried in his attache case and data on his laptop. The year had been good. Targets were met. Market share had increased and he had reason to be happy with the performance of his team. After hours of work on the Form, he was satisfied and shut it.

On Monday morning, he stepped out of his three-

The Golden Rule

bedroom first-floor apartment, ready for an eventful day at the office. Susan, his wife, closed the door firmly after she had waved him goodbye. He walked towards the elevator, changed his mind and unhurriedly took the steps to the porch. Joseph, his chauffeur over the last six years, let the black Honda Accord glide into the driveway. He scrambled out and held the rear door open. The six-foot frame of Alex Thomas slid into the rear seat. His bulging attache case sat snugly alongside.

The drive to the office would take twenty minutes; at times, a little longer. With meetings and discussions scheduled, Monday mornings were usually very busy; but today Alex Thomas was relatively tension-free. He sat back, unbuttoned his Armani Jacket, adjusted his sunglasses and smiled. He was looking forward to a good day. He knew that his appraisal would fetch him some positive remarks.

At 10.35 he was to meet his boss Victor Banerjee, the Chief Executive. Victor fixed odd times for discussions. It was never 10.30 or 11. It was rather 10.35 or 11.03. Why, Alex never knew. But 10.35, was okay. In fact he had set the morning aside for Victor.

Chapter 1 | The 360 Degree Appraisal

Joseph sensed the mood of his boss and quietly slipped in Vivaldi's Four Seasons. As notes from the speakers filled the car, Alex smiled again. Vivaldi's music for springtime was just right. He knew, as he got off at the office, there would be more than a spring in his step.

As Alex looked out, he noticed that malls were being decorated with festoons, buntings and Santa Claus. It was about three weeks to Christmas. He remembered that Antony his eight-year old son had planned to write to Santa Claus for a bicycle; the latest. 'Bright colors, curved handlebar and all that', in Antony's words. Alex knew that he must play Santa Claus latest by Christmas Eve.

At forty he was still young and very energetic; and looked it. He thrived on challenges, tight-corner situations, and relished the successes that followed. Not one to be laid-back and complacent, he accepted new tasks readily and involved himself fully. Perhaps Victor made note of the new initiatives he had taken lately.

He had joined the company as a young management trainee after his Post Graduation in Business Management. He

The Golden Rule

had opted for Marketing and did the rounds with field staff for months until he got his posting in Product Management. After that it was a steady climb: Assistant Product Manager, Product Manager, Regional Manager, Marketing Manager and now Vice-President, Marketing. He had no reason to complain. The company had been good to him.

The Honda came to a halt in the office parking area. As he stepped out, he noticed that Victor had not come in. His white Audi was not in its usual parking space. Victor always drove his car from and to the office, with the chauffeur perched on the edge of the rear seat. At the office the chauffeur took over. Why would a Chief Executive let his chauffeur sit watching, when he drove? Only Heaven knew. Victor was different in so many ways; not queer, but different; and it took time to understand him.

Alex walked to the elevator. Maya Mirchandani, was waiting in front of it. She greeted him.

"Will Mr Banerjee be in shortly?"

"10.29" confirmed Victor's secretary, "a meeting with Mr Ravi Kumar was scheduled at 9.25. He should be back after that."

"Thanks Maya."

They got into the elevator together. The ascent to the fourth floor was in silence.

Alex settled into his office. He called Sheila, his secretary, and quickly cleared papers which she had left on his desk on Friday evening. He made a few phone calls and hurriedly typed a few mails on his computer. It was 10.25. In ten minutes, his appraisal would start.

He seemed confident. With a track record that could not be faulted, he had little to worry. He had taken on competition at different times and often badly mauled it to boost his confidence. Yet this morning there was a suggestion of anxiety. This would the first appraisal after his promotion and he knew that Victor could keep one guessing. At 10.33 he left his office telling Sheila that he would be with the CEO, and moved into the passage leading to Victor's office. Sheila Jacob got busy with her work. When Alex Thomas was promoted last year, Sheila was moved from the regional office to the corporate office. She learnt fast and seldom kept work pending. Alex just loved that.

The Golden Rule

For him things had to be done now; right now.

Alex smiled as he passed Maya and moved into Victor's office. It was 10.35.

"Ah, you are here." Victor looked up.

"I better be here," Alex replied.

"Yes. Sit down Alex," Victor waved and continued, "The last time we talked of your appraisal we were flying over Delhi. That was just to remind ourselves that we had to talk."

"The time has come for us to talk." Alex sounded more like a Hyde Park Preacher as he handed Victor his appraisal form.

Victor pushed his chair back, crossed his legs, knotted his fingers, and looked Alex in the eye. "Alex, shall we set the appraisal form aside and just chat for awhile?"

Alex nodded.

"Tell me, how was this year?"

"The year is not over. We have figures up to November."

"Tell me more."

"Sales have grown by over 12%. Two new products

Chapter 1 | The 360 Degree Appraisal

launched have hit the jackpot. Market share is still climbing. The Traders are counting gains. And the team is happy. The score card looks respectable."

"That is good to hear. As always you enjoy the feel of success. Tell me more about your team."

"What would you want to know?"

"For starters, take this question: How have they accepted you?"

"You'll have to check that with them."

"No, I want your thoughts on it."

"Going by the way they respond to me, I should think they have no apparent grouse."

"Why would you say that?"

"I cannot read their minds."

"True. That is true."

"Rahul, Sunil and Lokesh seem to be okay with me."

"As your Marketing Managers do they see you as a strong and dependable leader or (he was looking for words), do they regard you as a boss who was once their peer; their friend?"

"I imagine I am both to them."

"Can you explain that?"

"A few years ago, I read a book titled Leadership and the One-Minute Manager. The authors write on situational management. You don't adopt a fixed style, they suggest. Instead you adapt to a situation. I found the idea eminently suitable. With Rahul, I delegate. With Sunil, I have to be supporting. With Lokesh, I have to be directing; more because he was promoted recently."

"I recall reading that book. Good stuff." Victor paused. And added, "But don't you have trouble adapting often?"

"Yes. In the beginning it was tough. It still is, but I am learning," Alex confided.

"Are you satisfied?" Victor persisted.

"It could always be better." Alex sounded cautious.

For the next twenty minutes or so they went over some others on the team and his peers. Victor showed signs of being pleased.

Chapter 1 | The 360 Degree Appraisal

"And how is it with the market?" Victor questioned.

"Right now things are reasonably good. With Regional Managers I meet the top customers every month. I visit the Traders and get feedback regularly. And I ensure that anything outside the ordinary comes to my attention immediately."

"Are you saying that you have set up a system for that?"

"You can say that."

"And how faithful is the system; how can you be sure?"

"I can never be absolutely sure. By and large it works."

Maya moved in ghost-like and left a tray with a gleaming tea pot and cups and disappeared. Victor rose and poured out tea into the two cups, offered one to Alex and sat back with his cup, perched on the edge of the table. They drank their tea in silence after Victor reassured Alex that he had asked for tea and not coffee, knowing his preference. The tea cups found their place back on the tray, and they got back to business.

"Alex. I am beginning to believe that our relationships, more than anything else, determine our success."

"And how do I score?" Alex probed.

The Golden Rule

"I'll come to that later," Victor deflected and continued: "Life is a network of relationships. And that is not a cliché."

"I am inclined to agree." Alex went along.

"And our relationships are only as good as our communication. This idea was proposed by John Powell, the celebrated Author. And I fully agree with him." Victor theorized.

Alex got the feeling that his appraisal was getting stalled. Victor was on a roll. And nobody stopped him when he decided to bounce ideas off you.

"You know, I have been doing some reading and some thinking. The time has come for me to share some thoughts with you."

Alex quickly looked at his watch. It was 11.40; an hour and twenty minutes to lunch. But he had set the morning aside for Victor. So he would have to stay and listen.

"Have you heard of the 360 Degree Appraisal?" Victor enquired.

"Yes. But I haven't given it much thought."

"Deepak, our HR man, is sold on it. I like the looks of it.

Chapter 1 | The 360 Degree Appraisal

In Business School it was only a topic. Now we have come face to face with it; to look at it seriously."

Opening his top drawer he pulled out the photocopy of an article. Very slowly and deliberately he gave it to Alex who had seen a similar article in a financial daily, but somehow did not get to read it. As Alex read the article, Victor called Maya. He wanted her to follow up on a few points. Then he dictated a message. Alex went through the illustration again.

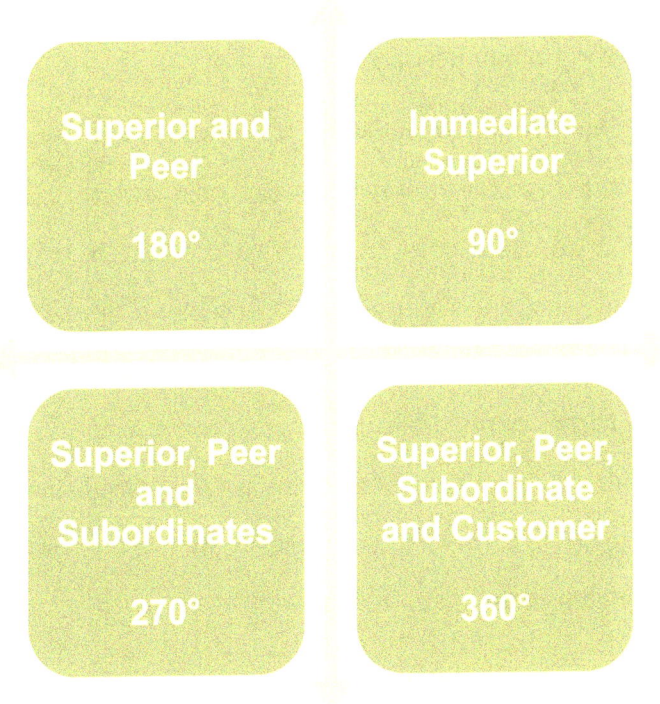

The Golden Rule

He thought that was a smart way of looking at relationships. Rather different from the old way of just getting feedback from only the superior. Check with different sources: The boss, the peer, the junior and the customer. Multi-source appraisal, looked fair.

Alex looked up. "Yes?" he quizzed.

"What do you think of it?" Victor asked.

"It seems good. But I do not recall how it works. Business School was a long time ago. And you know that I did not specialize in Human Resources."

"That is what we have to get Deepak to work on. I see a time in the near future when we can take a close look at it. Perhaps even use it here. In the West the System is popular, with many companies adopting it. The system is simple: instead of depending only on the evaluation by the boss, feedback is collected from peers, juniors and customers. The 360 degree appraisal is the sum total of all opinions. Graphically it appears in four segments. The boss continues to be the final judge, but after weighing the inputs from others."

"We should examine it. Check it out." Alex sounded

Chapter 1 | The 360 Degree Appraisal

reassuring.

"You know what we'll do? We'll put your appraisal on hold. Not for long, a few weeks perhaps."

Alex was not amused; but nodded.

"We'll set aside time for that. Maya will get back to you. Before that we have some serious talking to do."

"What is it about?" Alex asked with little interest.

"It is something that will affect our entire operations as professionals. We will have to look again at our roles to redefine them and choose a model to follow."

"You are into riddles. What exactly do you mean?"

"I was coming to that. We must meet; You, Deepak, the other VPs and I. I shall then share some thoughts with you."

"Very well then; just tell me when."

Alex rose to leave. Victor joined him at the door.

"Alex, set your worries aside on the appraisal. I know you have done well. I am putting off the exercise on purpose."

"If it's okay by you, it's okay by me." They shook hands

and parted.

Victor returned to his desk and called Maya. She entered as always, quietly.

"Maya will you line up a meeting with all the VPs? It is important. Also give them photocopies of this article." (The one he had shown Alex).

"Would Wednesday afternoon, 3:55 be okay with you?"

"You know my schedule. But how are they placed?"

"I have already checked that with the others. I have still to check with VP Marketing."

"It shall be 3:55 on Wednesday. Warn them that the session could be long."

"Yes sir."

Alex was pensive as he sat in the Honda on his way home. Joseph, who had the music discs numbered, sensed the mood and promptly slipped in the second movement of Beethoven's symphony No. 6; right for the pensive mood. Alex tried to put his thoughts together. Victor sounded very mystifying; talking in riddles; very unlike him. And yet he assured me that the appraisal was okay. Funny, Murphy's Law does work.

"Su," Alex turned to his wife as he sat sipping hot tea. "My appraisal has been put on hold."

"Why?" she was anxious.

"No problems. Victor said he would do it a few weeks later."

"But didn't he tell you why he put it off?"

"Yes. He wanted to discuss something very important with all of us."

"But surely it cannot be your performance."

"Not likely. The year has been good."

"Has he been reading some new book? Trying to bring in some new idea?"

"Yes; but it is early days yet." And added, "He said that it was okay; my appraisal I mean."

"If Victor said that, stop worrying. It should work out well. Your work will not go unnoticed."

Alex grinned. "Thank God, and thank you, Susan."

The Golden Rule

Chapter 2

The Relationship-Model

"What single ability do we all have? The ability to change."
~ L. Andrews.

Victor was a busy man. Crammed into each day was a tight schedule. With briefings, debriefings, a stream of mails and the rather continuous beep on his answer-phone, his diary was almost always packed. Tuesday was another busy day. Long meetings with Bill Foster, a contact from Singapore and with the Secretary of Industries, State Government, kept him fully occupied the whole day. On Wednesday, Andy, VP Finance and the Auditors met him in the morning. In the afternoon Victor was rather tense. He was preparing for his session with the VPs, scheduled for 3:55. He had done some homework, not very much though. At the meeting, he would kick start a thought-process; in fact two. He would have to watch for initial reactions before going into details. How would it go? He was uncertain.

The Golden Rule

Yet he decided to go ahead.

Maya walked in with a bunch of papers. He decided to check them right away. She waited. As she waited, her eyes fixed on the boss. He was graying at the temples. The top of his head had certainly seen better days. And, he was beginning to put on some weight. His five foot four was not that obvious because of his taste in clothes. His clothes, in a way, redeemed his appearance.

The man had been through tough days. Five years ago when he took over as CEO, he was a young 39. Nobody down the line believed he could turn things around. Figures were pathetic. Morale was low. Banks refused to meet people from the company who went asking for favors. It was a sorry plight. He came in like a breath of fresh air. Without complaining about the mess his predecessor had left, he set about expelling the stale air. The company needed oxygen and he brought with him loads of it; with his enthusiasm, energy, and courage. He was systematic, accessible, friendly, polite, ramrod straight and clear–headed. And he never gave up. He often quoted Churchill – Never, never, never, never give up. Today the company was endearingly called a blue-chip. There was a sense of well-being.

Chapter 2 | The Relationship-Model

Yet he believed his task was far from over. At forty-four, he had many dreams. The afternoon session would be the first of many, to make those dreams come true.

"Maya, nothing earth shaking, except for the message to Bruno. Will you please take this down and send it to him right away?" He gave her the bunch of papers and dictated a crisp reply. She was about to leave, when he stopped her.

"Maya, cheese sandwiches and coffee at 4:25 please. I know you will remember that VP Marketing likes tea, not coffee."

"Will there be anything else, sir?"

"Yes, none of us will be disturbed. Handle that for us".

"Yes sir."

Victor looked around his room. He felt good being the CEO; felt good the way things had gone over the past five years, although there were regrets over some mistakes; some mishaps that could have been avoided. He wished he could have looked at things from the start in the way he did in recent times. Perhaps changes could have been made earlier; perhaps the company could have achieved more. There was a tinge of sadness. Then he cast those depressing thoughts aside and felt the buzz of the present, even as he throbbed with enthusiasm and hope for the future. His eyes drifted to the message that hung over the door which read: "Never, never, never, never give up". He had not.

At 3:54 Maya peeped in to say that the VPs were waiting in her room. Could they come in? "Yes, of course!" he boomed.

Gaps, was the first to enter. The others followed. Victor shook each one by the hand and murmured, "Thank you. This is important." Quickly they found their seats in the corner of the CEO's office. Mini conferences were normally held here. Victor took his seat. Facing him were Gaps, Sammy, Andy, Deepak and Alex; the top five after him.

At 39, Gaps was relatively young. His rise was meteoric. He picked up degrees and diplomas in India, before doing a stint in the USA, where he amazed his employers with his vast knowledge and skill to unknot tangled ropes. He returned to India because of his father's failing health and joined the team as General Manager (Systems). Last year he became Vice-President. With an agile mind, he worked out options very fast, even in a crisis; was proactive and therefore a step ahead. What endeared him to others was his willingness to help those in need of his skills.

Sammy, now past 48, started at the bottom, on the shop floor. Diligently he worked his way up, learning fast and well, and acquiring a Master's degree in Political Science, not to be left out in the area of formal education. He read much and participated in every local seminar on manufacturing and materials. He was a 'seasoned professional' in the eyes of his peers. He knew his area of work and gained the respect of even competitors.

Andy was a Chartered Accountant with over twenty years of experience in Finance. They said he knew his subject. The auditors genuinely respected his knowledge and the bankers paid heed to his suggestions. It was rumored that he could check financial statements and spot flaws with ease; his team vouched for that. With his background he could find a place in any top team. At 45 he looked very secure.

Suave and sophisticated; that was Deepak Chopra. At 42 he had achieved much. He spent a few years in England where

The Golden Rule

he acquired a fine taste in ties; stripes and spots only. He was always well groomed and courteous. In England working in the area of Human Resources he got a world view of this developing discipline. He was open to new ideas, and had some fresh ideas of his own.

Alex Thomas was the closest; a friend.

Victor surveyed the group again and smiled; a disarming smile. "Gentlemen," he began, "today could see the birth of a great idea in your company. For that your company needs your total cooperation. First, try to understand the idea. Second, give me your studied feedback. How we respond to the idea could determine the path it takes. Please feel free to speak your mind, once the idea is in the open." He found them shifting in their seats, uncomfortable with the uncertainty. But they knew that with Victor they could speak their minds. Be frank; even blunt. Relationships would not suffer.

"On Monday morning, the day before yesterday, Alex and I sat down to discuss his appraisal. We did not finish the exercise. We shall be at it soon enough. During the discussion, we touched on an idea doing the rounds in some companies in

Chapter 2 | The Relationship-Model

India – the 360 degree appraisal. You have with you some reading material that Maya sent you. Each company employee, starting with me, should be appraised against feedback from his superior, his peers, his juniors and his customers. Put differently appraisal only by the boss is no more enough. We need to know how we are seen by others with whom we transact. We need to assess our relationships, because it is believed that the stronger the relationship, the better the transaction. And we are transacting constantly; with seniors, juniors, peers and external agencies. By now you know that the System is popular in the West." Victor stopped. There was silence. No one wanted to be the first to break it. He did.

"So far, we have not had professional feedback from anyone but the boss. That system was useful for a time. The time has come for a new idea. Perhaps Deepak could set the discussion in motion."

Deepak warmed to the idea. "I have some data. Not enough. I am trying to get more information from companies in India who have initiated the 360 degree appraisal. Not many are into it yet. But preliminary findings are encouraging. Those who have tried it, find some merit in it. In England I had the opportunity to introduce the system in the company I worked. In India, the situation will not be the same. Tradition and cultural factors are different and drastic changes are difficult to make. By and large, we Indians do not take kindly to negative feedback. We resent suggestions on how to improve. In short, we are slow to change. Therefore, we will have many hurdles to cross, if the system is to be introduced."

Gaps, was the next to respond. "It has a new angle to it, which appeals to reason. Some American companies I know have the system working for them."

Sammy: "Would this go down to the shop floor?"

Victor: "We don't know yet."

"The factory worker does not interact with customers and agencies," Sammy continued.

Deepak: "Yes. We'll have to reckon with that."

Andy: "What's the catch? What are the hassles?"

"Count on the finance guy to look for loop holes," Alex joked.

Andy: "Shouldn't we approach it with caution?"

Chapter 2 | The Relationship-Model

Victor: "Of course with abundant caution!"

Alex: "To me the idea looks good; especially for marketing people. We only talk of customer satisfaction and customer delight. Only lip service. We really do not get specific feedback from customers. This could be one way of doing it."

Victor: "You certainly have a point there. We have been shoddy in getting organized feedback from customers."

Andy: "Are you saying that increments and promotions will be based on such feedback?"

Deepak: "As I said earlier, In India we will have to adapt the System. That is why it is too early to answer that. But the CSI and ESI are likely to be reckoning points".

Sammy: "What's that?

Deepak: "CSI stands for Customer Satisfaction Index and ESI is for Employee Satisfaction Index. The whole idea is to treat everyone we interact with as a customer: Customers, suppliers, all agencies, the boss, peers, juniors and so on. We broadly divide all such customers into two categories: The external customer and the internal customer. Unless the internal

The Golden Rule

customer is satisfied, he may not satisfy the external customer. So, all round satisfaction is important. Building relationships with all segments is important. Assessing how those relationships impact each one's performance is important. Let me read you two appropriate quotations: 'I firmly believe you cannot become a 100% customer-focused company until you've become a 100% employee-focused company. But the converse is also true. If you become a 100% employee-focused company, you almost certainly will become a 100% customer-focused company'. It is from the book Stop Paddling and Start Rocking the Boat, by Lou Prichett. And the second quotation reads: 'I have never seen a company that was able to satisfy its customers that did not also satisfy its employees. Your employees will treat your customers no better than you treat your employees'. Those were the words of Larry Bossidy, erstwhile CEO of Honeywell. Very simply it means overall improvement in People Management: People inside the company; and people outside the company who transact with the company. Thompson, of Templeton College, Oxford, and Richardson, of the London School of Economics, presented a review of the most authoritative literature on the subject of

People Management. The thirty-odd studies showed that good people management practices worked wonders for the bottom line."

Andy: "I like the part on improving bottom lines. Otherwise the idea is rather complex. We better tread carefully."

Victor: "You can say that again. One purpose of this meeting is to acquaint you with the idea. If you agree that the idea is worth investigating, Deepak will go into details and get back to us."

Alex: "With me it's go-go."

Gaps: "Nothing wrong in checking it out."

Sammy: "Check. But let us be discreet. We don't want the shop floor thinking that we are devising a tool to get rid of some of them."

Victor: "You can be sure that Deepak will handle it prudently."

Deepak: "Thank you, Victor. I'll do what I can."

Andy: "Are we fixing any time-frame for the investigation?"

Victor: "I think we'll leave that to Deepak."

Deepak: "About four to six weeks for some preliminary information."

Victor: "That should be fine. We shall look at it in the third week of January."

The sandwiches were fast disappearing from the tray; so were the coffee and tea. Maya came in at 4:25, as scheduled.

Was the meeting over? Had Victor anything else to say? Each looked at the other.

Victor cleared his throat, in an attempt to gain time. And ventured: "What do you think of Jesus? Jesus Christ?"

The group looked at him in surprise.

Gaps, very strong in his Hindu beliefs, questioned: "What has Jesus got to do with us?"

A shocked Sammy was more guarded when he said: "We have heard of him."

Andy: "I am not sure how that question is relevant to our discussion on the 360 Degree Appraisal."

Chapter 2 | The Relationship-Model

Victor: "Thank you Andy. You have given me the right lead. We spoke of the 360 Degree Appraisal and relationships. It is said that Jesus is a model for relationship-building. We professionals, can we learn something from him?"

Alex: "Let us leave Jesus out of this. He is a Religious Head and he better stay so."

Victor: "Are you suggesting that religion and business are water-tight compartments?"

Alex was apologetic. "Not really. But they are better, when left alone."

Victor: "Should not our beliefs guide us in our business; in our profession? Should they not shape the way we act, react and interact?"

Alex: "That goes without saying."

Victor: "Why then this fear? That apart, I am not suggesting that we look at Jesus as a Religious Head. We shall not get into the spiritual side of Jesus, the Divine Powers, he is said to have had. We plan to look at him as a man, as a Professional and a leader of his times. Is there something that

The Golden Rule

we can learn from him? If we can learn from Jack Welch and Bill Gates why not learn from Jesus?"

Andy: "Jack Welch and Bill Gates were managers of our time. We see them in the current context. Jesus lived 2000 years ago. He seems ancient."

Victor: "You are right. He is an old-time leader and Professional. But can he give all-time leaders and professionals nuggets of wisdom? Could an American President of the 21st century look back at Abraham Lincoln and learn a thing or two? Or would he say that Lincoln is ancient? The way I see it, Jesus is not ancient. Jesus is ageless."

Deepak: "That was cleverly said."

Victor: "Thank you Deepak. Is that not the situation? All I ask of us is to be open. Can we shed our inhibitions and fears and look at Jesus, just as we would look at say, Steve Jobs, Ratan Tata or the Ambani brothers? How did he manage things 2000 years ago? Are there lessons for us? We shall not, I repeat, even remotely get involved in his Divinity."

Deepak: "To me that sounds fair."

Chapter 2 | The Relationship-Model

Victor: "Let me share something with you that only Pamela, my wife, knows. About six months ago I was in Delhi. I had to stay there for four days. I had nothing to read. Looking around the hotel room I spotted a copy of the Holy Bible. With nothing else to do I began reading the New Testament - The Gospel of St .Mathew. By the time I got to chapter 5, I was hooked. I read through Mathew; all 28 chapters. I finished a late meal and went out for a stroll.

What struck me was the incredible responsiveness of the central character – Jesus – to his environment, the people, the happenings, the traditions, the practices. He was so alive to what happened around him that he was not caught off guard. The Gospel of Mathew is a fascinating study of a magnetic personality. The next evening out of sheer curiosity I read the Gospel of St. Mark; though I returned to the hotel only after 7. During the next two evenings I read through Luke and John. I was enthralled; absolutely captivated. In the Gospels, four writers record the life, words and works of Jesus Christ. And I had read all the four – Mathew, Mark, Luke and John.

What I understood from the Gospels was that Jesus was a Professional hidden to man, who needed to come out of those pages and address us. I came back and bought myself a copy of the Holy Bible. I read the 4 Gospels again and yet again. I have read them four times. I am looking forward to my fifth attempt. My wife, who is a Christian, explained some passages to me. Later, I met a few people who helped me clarify some of my doubts. Fr. Eric D' Cruz, the Principal at my son's school was very helpful. He listened to me; spent much time with me; and gave me relevant reading material. I found the material enlightening. At the end of this study I placed before myself a proposition, which I place before you: Can Jesus give us a new way; a new template for running our business?"

An uncomfortable silence descended on the group as each looked at the others to spot signals that would dispel their fear: were they going religious?

It was Maya who broke the silence as she looked in. "Is there anything you need sir? May I get you some more coffee, perhaps?" Victor looked around. No one spoke. "No thank you, Maya." As she stood there his eyes signaled her on some action.

Deepak spoke up at last: "I was not in the least prepared for such a turn in the discussions. But I see your point. We lose nothing by looking at a great man and checking if we can learn something from him."

Alex: "Let's keep religion out."

Gaps: "I'm not too sure. I shall have to think over this strange situation. As of now, it sounds odd."

Andy: "Same here."

Sammy: "I think Deepak took the words out of my mouth: Why not?"

Victor: "If there is some readiness to examine the idea I shall give you some reading material."

Deepak: "That should be a good beginning." He rose to collect the papers that Victor held out. Each set had a collection of five articles that were titled:

- The Source – The Gospels
- The Age and Times
- The Fully Human Professional
- Relationship with the Team

The Golden Rule

- Jesus and Professionals

Victor: "I thought we should begin with these articles to understand the basics; to understand the circumstances in which Jesus operated. Jesus did not manufacture and market products, as we do. He promoted a concept. How he did that is what we shall look at. Let me call out a few lines from Mahatma Gandhi: 'Of all things I have read what remained with me forever, was that Jesus came almost to give a new law – not an eye for an eye but to receive two blows when only one was given, and to go two miles when they were asked to go one. It is the sermon that endeared Jesus to me'. Gandhi, whom we respect, lived and died a Hindu; but he was not averse to reading the Gospels and getting to know Jesus. For those of us who have reservations on reading the Gospels that thought should be comforting." He paused for a moment to let the idea sink in, and continued: "Once you have read the material we could meet on Friday. Would that suit you?"

Alex: "Friday morning is out. I am in the market. Friday afternoon should be okay with me."

The others had no words, but nodded. The group

Chapter 2 | The Relationship-Model

disbanded after Victor thanked them profusely for their time and participation.

As they returned to their offices they found a copy of the New Testament and a note which read:

"You are shocked. Please do not feel guilty. I understand. We are professionals who shall not fear checking options. Check this option, I implore you. If it is promising we pursue. If not, we drop it. Please find time to read the New Testament (Gospels) and the additional sheets. Knowing you, I can promise you one result – you'll enjoy it. Read the New Testament like you would read Stephen R. Covey or Tom Peters or your favorite management author. Disregard the religion in it. Do we consider the religious beliefs of Covey or Peters when we read them? We take in only the professional insights. In the same way, look for life-changing clues in the material I have given you. I am going to count on your doing just that. I am going to count on your ushering in change.

May the best of your past, be the worst of your future.
-Victor."

The Golden Rule

Chapter 3
The Source – The Gospels

"When love and skill work together, expect a Masterpiece."

~ C. Read.

Jesus was not keen on documenting his words and deeds. That is why he discouraged even those who were healed, from circulating information on the healing they experienced. The only reference to his act of writing is in John 8:6 - "Jesus bent down and wrote with his finger on the ground." But others wrote of him, his words, his deeds and his short life. An authentic account is found in what is popularly called The Gospels. Four writers put down facts and their commentary. There is much in common in their narratives, but each is different in its own way. Mathew and John were two of his twelve apostles. Mark and Luke were disciples of his apostles. Together the four have portrayed Jesus for all time.

MATHEW (28 chapters)

The Golden Rule

With Rome reigning over Palestine, tax collection was the extorting face of the emperor in the land he occupied, and tax collectors were his crafty emissaries who did his bidding. Mathew, one such tax collector, was seen as a stooge of the Rome. Like others in his trade, he was exploited by the Romans and despised by the Jews. Yet when Jesus, a Jew, called him he left everything and followed him to become a loyal apostle.

In his Gospel he sets out to prove an audacious claim: Jesus Christ is the very Messiah, promised in the Old Testament - *Christ* is the Greek translation of the word *Messiah*. The Old Testament, as we know it, is an account of the lives, hopes and travails of the Jewish people before the birth of Christ. Epic stories in the Old Testament were lessons for the Jews, who listened to them often to affirm their faith in the coming of the Savior, which was foretold by many prophets.

The Jews eagerly waited for the Messiah, the Promised One. His coming would change things, they believed. Could Jesus be the long awaited Messiah? To answer that question, Mathew starts with a genealogy. Mathew does not begin with Christ's birth. Instead he reaches further back to establish his roots. He traces his lineage to the father of the Jewish race, Abraham.

Chapter 3 | The Source – The Gospels

After recording Jesus' bloodline, Mathew narrates the story of his life on earth. He relies heavily on the Old Testament, quoting frequently from it, because he was writing mainly for the Jews, who believed in the Old Testament.

What does a Tax collector like? Organized and neatly documented figures, with all types of tax accounted for. Mathew, the tax collector, turned apostle, did precisely that: organized thinking, in topically grouping facts. First, in chapters 5-7, he inspires the reader through the famous Sermon on the Mount. Second, in chapter 10, he records the instructions Jesus gave his disciples on their mission. Third, in chapter 13, he lists a series of parables on the kingdom which Jesus tells his listeners. Fourth, in chapter 18, he records Jesus' words on the Church as a community. Fifth, in chapters 23-25, he describes Jesus' anger when he denounces hypocrisy. In the same chapters (23-25) he writes of the predictions Jesus makes on the future. The reader cannot but notice some order in his reporting. The reader also spots stories on money, natural to a tax collector.

Many important leaders work hard to convey an impression of confidence and power. A leader, they assume, should look like a leader; dress like one; behave like one; and project the image of one who is powerful. With the right image he could attract crowds. In sharp contrast, Mathew depicts Jesus as the leader who broke stereotypes. He had power, enormous power; but he used power with compassion. He thought less of how others appraised him. Instead, he cared more for the needs of others and what he could do for them.

His leadership had many facets. One was distinctly seen as he neared Jerusalem, the capital city. He let the people take him through one moment of public triumph with much wild cheering and exultation. Even in such a hero's welcome, he rode not a stallion, but a donkey colt. And a few days later he left his followers a lasting sign of shame and humiliation – the Cross; the sign of Roman punishment. Mathew shows how Jesus was composed in triumph and stoic in tribulation.

Jesus opened his ministry in his hometown, in a synagogue, a place of worship and discourse; an occasion that ended almost in a riot. When he returned to his hometown after visiting other towns, he aroused great curiosity, but little belief. The locals could not understand how, one raised in their town by a carpenter could now teach them like a Rabbi. Some close to him even called him Master. How could this be? Mathew unravels the paradox deftly.

He recounts some of the growing tensions between Jesus and the groups that resisted him; they followed him from town to town, setting traps for him. How did Jesus respond? Not by getting incensed, but by using the occasions of conflict to caution his disciples and the crowds who followed him, against the trickery of these troublemakers. He was not trapped with their bait; instead he had them hooked on their own line that Mathew 22:46 concludes: "From that day, no one dared to ask him any more questions." The Pharisees, the Scribes and the Sadducees, who were important sects, found in Jesus a formidable opponent. Continuing with the same theme in Chapter 23, Mathew records Jesus' eloquent verdict on the Pharisees. Jesus rebuked them for being proud and petty, and for refusing to admit their wrongs. Outward, showy observances, Jesus said, tend to divert attention away from a person's inner growth. And he went on to caution them that hypocrisy put distance between them and the common people.

Mathew's Gospel depicts the multi-faceted personality of Jesus so well, that the French sceptic Renan praised this

The Golden Rule

Gospel as "the most important book of Christendom – the most important that has ever been written".

MARK (16 chapters)

Mark probably got his facts from Peter, the apostle. And with those facts set about writing a fast paced Gospel: clear, well edited, with little scope for dialogue and reflection, but full of action. Adopting a rather unconventional style of writing, he records the impact of a historical figure, on his times. Jesus provoked strong reactions in everyone. He aroused fierce opposition among his own neighbors and among the religious die-hards. But the common people were amazed.

No Gospel writer describes the physical appearance of Jesus. Mark succeeds in painting a picture of his humanity: A very normal human being, compassionate to those in need, but angry at the hard-hearted response of his opposition. He was dismayed at the tricky questions that came from the suspicious religious leaders and troubled at their disbelief, although he excelled in repartee and logical debate. When he was weary he wanted quiet and peace, away from the crowds. There were times he felt lonely and disappointed; and times when he was unashamed to weep for the sorrows of others.

Mark captures in words, a spectrum of human emotions that Jesus showed. Take this, for example: in Jerusalem Jesus is surrounded by hostile groups. In Chapter 12, Mark records a series of attempts made by the Pharisees, Sadducees and others to trap him. The intelligent and forthright manner in which he accepts and meets those challenges makes interesting reading - case study in people management.

During much of his ministry, Jesus tried to dissuade people from praising his extraordinary powers and wondrous works. But in a rare scene Mark depicts large crowds recognizing him as the Messiah and honoring him. In subsequent chapters, Mark recounts how the same crowds humiliate and disgrace him. He clearly demonstrates how short-lived public applause is. At the time of Jesus' death, the dramatic climax, Jerusalem is packed with people from all over the region. They are there for the Passover - a celebration of the time Jews were delivered from Egypt. Mark concludes that Jesus could not have chosen a better time to end his promising life. Like an experienced editor, Mark cuts and puts together pieces that read like an engrossing and exciting biography.

The Golden Rule

LUKE (24 chapters)

It is unlikely that Luke knew Jesus personally. But as a dedicated convert in the early Church, he accompanied the apostle Paul (who was not among the twelve apostles Jesus chose, but who joined the group after the death of the Master). In three of his letters, Paul refers to Luke with great affection.

Luke's Gospel is like a musical - a Greek Musical, composed by one who was hugely gifted. The mouth opens in song when the heart is full of joy; and the tempo does not drop. In his introduction, Luke stresses the need to draw up a carefully researched account of Jesus' life and works. So, he gathers information from eyewitnesses. Scholars assume that he could have interviewed even Mary, mother of Jesus, to get his facts on the early life of her son. If Mark's gospel is one of action, Luke's is a gospel of relationships. It unfolds very good character descriptions.

Among the Gospel writers, only Luke dated the events by referring to Roman Emperors. He was determined to write a thorough and factual account, which included dating events in their historical context. Mathew's gospel traced Jesus' roots back to Abraham, father of the Jewish race. But Luke, the only non-Jew writer of the gospels, emphasized that Jesus' good news was for all people, not just for the Jews. To prove that point he traced Jesus' lineage all the way to Adam.

Luke, a physician, knew first-hand about sick and suffering people. That explains the inclusion of physical healing and repeated reference to Jesus' compassion for the afflicted. Luke shows him as a true servant of all humanity. Jesus avoided such fashionable places as the resort town, Tiberias. He stayed near the farming communities and fishing villages around the Sea of Galilee, serving ordinary people. Different sections of people came to him. Each for a different reason: The sick, wanting healing; the hungry, hoping to be fed; the confused seeking clarity; and even the rich and the powerful (the Roman Centurion, the Ruler of a synagogue and the Chief Tax Collector) imploring favors. He listened to each and empathized. Luke traces these encounters with a rare diligence.

Women, largely ignored by ancient historians, play a large role in Luke's gospel. He introduces thirteen women, not mentioned by other gospel writers; and he delights in including children in his narrative.

The Golden Rule

Jesus opposed the legalism and the blinkered views of some of the Jews. For example, some of them observed very strict rules governing the Sabbath. Jesus broke those rules. How? By helping people on the Sabbath, he explained to them that rules should not come in the way of succoring the needy. He refused to let traditions stop him from reaching out to those in distress. And what was the Jewish response? They were furious that he flouted their edicts, and would not rest until they hatched a plot to seize and kill him. They would not let even Pilate, the Roman Governor, foil that plot.

Luke, master story-teller, records eighteen parables that appear nowhere else, even as he includes some of the more familiar. While Mathew emphasizes parables of the kingdom, Luke adds those that focus on people: The Good Samaritan, the Lost Coin and the Prodigal Son are some. In the parable of the Good Samaritan, the priest saw the waylaid victim in a half-dead state. According to the Old Testament Law, a priest who touched a dead body, made himself unclean. Therefore the priest and the religious Levite decided not to get involved. The audience listening to the parable would have expected Jesus to introduce a third character, perhaps a Jew. But Jesus gave the story a twist.

The third character, who stopped to help and show love, was not a Jew, but a Samaritan, a minority, despised by the Jews. In this parable Jesus showed that the brotherhood of man did not recognize boundaries or limits; it embraced humankind.

Through his teachings and actions Jesus showed how relationships could be built and sustained. Luke's gospel records those lessons.

JOHN (21 chapters)

John deviated sharply from the other three. They focused on events. He concentrated on the meaning of what Jesus said and did. John's Gospel is a result of great reflection. Using simple words Jesus conveyed great meaning. John's Gospel is full of those simple words that Jesus used eloquently.

Many specific details show that he was an eyewitness. He describes the stone water jars at Cana, where Jesus changed water into wine (2:6). He refers to Nicodemus who was a prominent Pharisee, a group violently opposed to Jesus. This Pharisee knew it was not prudent to meet Jesus during the day, so he chose to meet him at night and in secret (3:2). Two other remarks on Nicodemus show that Jesus had a strong influence on him. He stood up for Jesus at the Jewish Ruling Council (7:50) and helped prepare Jesus' body for burial (19:39). Jesus' meeting with a Samaritan woman (4:4-42) probably had the same kind of intrigue as his forced encounter with the woman caught in adultery (8:3-11). A dialogue between a Jew and a Samaritan, let alone between a Rabbi and an adulteress, was taboo. Yet John highlights these encounters to emphasize Jesus' mission. He even records the exact number of fish caught by the apostles (21:11). John does not leave out the details which add to the credibility of his account.

The first six chapters unfold the identity of Jesus. The next six contrast the increasingly divided opinion on Jesus. On the one hand, his disciples were won over and Jesus gained a loyal following among the people. On the other hand, his enemies rejected all the evidence he presented. Ultimately their hatred spilled over and the venom was strong enough to kill. The remaining chapters fathom the depth of Jesus' words and actions.

John omits many of the events recorded in Mark; many of the long speeches recorded in Mathew, and the parables of Luke. Instead John pictures close-ups of people who responded to Jesus: some who followed him openly; others who were suspicious; and some others who were hostile.

Although Mathew, Mark and Luke record miracles, John goes one step further and calls them signs. A sign points to something. In John, supernatural acts are one more proof of Jesus' unique nature. Jesus refused to perform miracles as magic to dazzle the crowds, but used them instead as object lessons.

That Jesus' life went even beyond what is recorded in the Gospels is clear in John 21:24-25: "This is the disciple who is testifying to these things and has written them, and we know that his testimony is true. But there are also many other things that Jesus did; if every one of them were written down, I suppose that the world itself could not contain the books that would be written". A hyperbole all right, but the point is taken. There was more wonder in his life than recorded in the gospels; Jesus was too big to be confined to the pages of a text, or caged between the covers of a book.

Through Mathew who highlights the public utterances of Jesus, Mark who unfolds his humanity, Luke who treats Jesus' relationships with sensitivity, and John who explains the

The Golden Rule

meaning of His words and acts, we see the person of Jesus. In short, the Gospels provide an action plan for relationships. Jesus clearly establishes that his teachings can be practiced and that his people-management principles are for all time.

Chapter 4
The Age and Times

"Men build too many walls; and not enough bridges."

~ D. Pire

The period in which we live is important, because it impacts the way we think and act. Circumstances are significant and our responses to them are more significant. That is why a political leader is assessed against the turbulent times in which he leads his people; a corporation is gauged by the exacting conditions in which it operates and a professional is appraised in the context of the tough environment in which he works. To understand the role that Jesus played and its relevance, it is necessary to examine the age and times in which he lived and worked.

Jesus was born in Circa 7 B.C. (some scholars suggest 4 B.C.) in a stable in Bethlehem, an obscure village in Palestine. His mother was Jewish. He grew up like an ordinary Jewish child.

The Golden Rule

Later, he worked as a carpenter, among Jews. When he turned 30, he started his public ministry among the Jewish people. For 3 years he went about this ministry with a rare dedication. When he was 33 he was crucified and put to death by the Jews; the Romans were incidental. During his 33 years he did not hold any public office, except being referred to as Rabbi – which is teacher. He did not have a family of his own, or own a house, or have any possessions, but for the clothes he wore. He did not travel more than 200 miles from where he was born. He had no credentials but himself.

Such a sketchy reference to his life does him no justice. It does the four gospel writers no justice either. The purpose of the brief account is to stress the Jewish parameters. He was born a Jew, brought up as one, lived as one. He had to operate in Jewish conditions and cope with the contradictions the system bred. There seemed no escape. What were these Jewish conditions? Let us consider the Jewish race, to begin with.

THE JEWS

The Jews, as a people, were subjugated by the Romans. The yoke was heavy and the labor hard. Some chose to rebel and revolt, but most suffered in silence, because they waited for a Messiah, the Promised One, who was foretold by the Prophets. This Promised One, the Messiah would liberate them from bondage. They believed he would come and trample the enemy underfoot, leading them to a long-awaited victory. So there was hope and great expectation.

There were many groups. They spoke the same language (though in numerous dialects), believed in the same law and prophets and worshipped at the same temple; yet they were in a state of strife. Their strong rivalry paralyzed any joint effort against the Romans.

Prominent among them were the Pharisees - the puritans of that time. They were law-enforcing, law-abiding, pretentious and sanctimonious humbugs. They wore gaunt and hungry looks during a brief fast, prayed grandiosely if people watched and went so far as to strap verses from the law books on their left arms and foreheads. For them the letter of the law, and not the spirit, was important; the law given to them by Prophet Moses. The thought of foreign domination was revolting, yet they chose to be peaceful as long as the Romans did not interfere in their religious observances. They explained away the bondage as God-ordained. The belief that the Messiah would come and deliver them, sustained them in difficult times. When he did come, he would dispense key positions to them in the new government; so they hoped. Students of history have often puzzled over the friction between the Pharisees and Jesus. At first glance, he should have liked them because they were the most religious group of that time. Yet their over-legalistic behavior cast doubts on their motives, prompting Jesus to say: "They do not practice what they teach" Matt 23:3.

The Scribes were a sub-sect of the Pharisees. They were the law experts. People in doubt went to them and they explained the law and clarified doubts. This was a vital function because the entire Jewish community was law-bound. The knowledge they had, conferred on the Scribes, a right to high positions in the Synagogue and the Sanhedrin, important institutions of that time.

Despite their duplicity, the Pharisees had the support of the common people, to fight another class known as the Sadducees. The Sadducees refused to accept the interpretation of the law given by the Scribes (Pharisees). For them only the first five books of the Old Testament were important; the other books were disputed. They were aristocrats, materialistic and politically well connected. They lobbied with the Romans to gain key positions.

The Levites were the priestly order, meant to hold priestly office. But, with the Sadducees occupying the top priestly positions, the Levites were relegated to lower levels in the hierarchy.

The Zealots were a group of extremists. They believed that only by armed revolt could the Romans be overthrown. They looted and plundered to finance their armed rebellion. Fury apart, they could not hold out for long. The Romans crushed the rebellion and squeezed out any residual hope they nursed. Barabbas, the criminal, whom Pilate offered as a trade-off for Jesus, was a Zealot. So were the criminals, on crosses on either side of Jesus when he was crucified at Calvary.

The Herodians were a political sect which pledged support to Herod, the King of Judea. Though a king, he too was subject to Rome. His followers indulged in political intrigue and excelled in wheeling and dealing. The King was at home in their company and enjoyed the flattery that the sycophants lavished on him.

The Publicans were contractors engaged by the Romans to collect taxes. They were a hated group, because they collected more than was specified, and kept the difference. Matthew, the apostle, came from this group.

The Samaritans, referred to in the parables, were social outcasts. The Jews, by and large, had nothing to do with them. Anyone interacting with them was despised, including Jesus who tried to reach out to them.

In all the groups, women and children hardly had a say. Men decided; women and children just obeyed. This ostracism in the decision-making process went so far as to forbid women from receiving religious instructions in the Torah, the five books of Moses, the great prophet. A Rabbi is known to have remarked: "rather should the words of the Torah be burnt, than entrusted to a woman".

Jesus was concerned with the social oppression of women. He had very positive views on women and engaged them publicly in discussion. The Samaritan woman at the well, Martha and Mary, and other women introduced in his parables were examples. Jesus understood the plight of widows, who were oppressed and helpless (Luke 7:12-13). In taking up the cause of women, he was strikingly original for his time. He offered a new way of relating that transcended divisions of rich and poor, slave and free, man and woman. He proposed the making of a new community, opposed to the enthroning of the individual or the exalting of any group. "American culture encourages the individual to 'be all you can be'. Yet this extraordinary strength, leaves America vulnerable, because it ignores the needs of the larger community upon which even the strongest individual must depend. Individualism is half the solution only." - an extract from: The Seven Cultures of Capitalism, Charles Hampden Turner and Fons Trompnaars. Jesus anticipated and promoted this paradigm shift two thousand years ago.

THE INSTITUTIONS

The several Jewish groups who were at strife, vied for honors in the celebrated institutions of that time - The Synagogue, The Sanhedrin, The Temple.

The Synagogue was the Jewish place of worship and

The Golden Rule

religious teaching. Prayers were offered, discourses were held and doubts clarified in this holy place. It was in one such Synagogue that Jesus began his public ministry.

The Sanhedrin was the highest Jewish court – the ruling council or assembly. It was made up of 70 (some experts place the number at 71) prominent citizens. The High Priest was the head of the Sanhedrin. The members belonged to 3 groups. The first was the Chief Priest group. They were prominent members drawn from families of former high priests and the current high priest. The second group, known as Ancients, comprised the wealthy and influential members of the laity. The third group came from the Scribes, the doctors of the law. Even though the Romans had conquered Palestine and a Roman government ruled the colony, the Jews were allowed to address many of their own problems. The Sanhedrin had the powers to decide whether someone was innocent or guilty of breaking a Jewish law. The temple Police enforced the pronouncements of the Sanhedrin. But the council could not put to death a person found guilty, without the permission of the Roman Governor. That is why Pilate, the Roman Governor, had to be persuaded to pronounce the death sentence on Jesus. The Jews could only manipulate the situation to their advantage.

The Temple of Jerusalem, to the Jews of that time, was like Mecca to the Muslims of today – the holiest of holies. Even those who lived far away dreamed of a time when they would visit the temple and worship there. A good number made the visit once a year. Entry to the inner areas was restricted only to the Jews; transgressors were threatened with death. Women had limits marked out; beyond those they could not proceed. Because of the need for offering sacrifice – either for supplication or by way of penance – the sale of birds and sacrificial animals was brisk. Traders jostled to gain prime spots and moneychangers did good business. Such trading peaked at festival time when hundreds of thousands converged on the temple. To cater to these worshippers priests were necessary - at one time 24,000 of them were operating at the temple, vying for clientele and compensation. Although there was some division of labor among the priests, the more privileged functions were assigned to the high priests, who were Sadducees. The system automatically made them head of the Sanhedrin. The clout they enjoyed was enormous. They could make or break careers; and lives. With more and more people

The Golden Rule

coming under the sway of Jesus' teaching, they feared that they would be sidelined soon. They could not let that happen and decided to break the stronghold Jesus had.

At Jesus' arrest the religious and political leaders got a close look at him. They had heard of his miraculous powers and hoped he would perform for them like a magician. He had no such pact with them. Silently and firmly he declined. Not even with his life at stake would he humour them, bewitch them with miracles because he shunned the spectacular. He would use his powers only to help the needy.

The Gospels record a pass-the-buck sequence in Jesus' encounter with Jewish and Roman justice. The Sanhedrin judged Jesus guilty of blasphemy, but it did not have the authority to carry out the death sentence. They needed Pilate. So they sent Jesus to Pilate. Along the way they changed the religious charge against Jesus into a political charge, which alone would prompt the governor to take action. Pilate shunted Jesus to Herod, the king of Judea, who had jurisdiction over the home region of Jesus. Herod taunted and mocked Jesus, and then sent him back to Pilate. Three times Pilate tried to release Jesus, but fear of offending Caesar, the Emperor, finally made him yield to the mob which was manipulated puppet-like, by vested interests.

LANGUAGE AND TRADE

Although Rome ruled, Greek influence was apparent. Next to Aramaic (a Hebrew dialect) Greek was the most widely used language. Luke wrote his gospel in Greek. It was also the language of commerce. And commerce was buoyant.

Palestine, at that time, was among the more prosperous occupations in the Roman Empire. Wheat and barley grew in abundance. Surplus grain went to Rome and to the other parts of the empire. Fruit, olives, figs, dates and timber were traded in, and business thrived.

THE SABBATH

The Jews observed the Sabbath in the strictest manner possible. They almost deified the day. The day started at sunset on Friday and ended at sunset on Saturday. It was set aside for Divine worship. The best clothes were worn. The best food eaten (cooked of course, the previous day). Physical work was restricted. The Sabbath day law listed many different physical activities that were prohibited. For example, walking beyond 3000 feet at a stretch was not allowed. Even the weight of

The Golden Rule

articles to be lifted was specified. On the Sabbath a man could ride a donkey. But if he used a whip to speed up the animal, he would be found guilty of laying a burden on it. Alms to a beggar could be given, on the Sabbath, only if he stuck his hand inside the home of the Pharisee, who would not have to extend his arm. A woman was forbidden from looking into the mirror. She might spot a gray hair and may be tempted to pluck it out – an activity that was ill-advised. The fanatical observances of the Sabbath were so extreme that the Jews refused to do battle on the Sabbath, even in self-defense of their country. That gave the Romans reason not to recruit Jews into the Roman regiments stationed in Palestine.

The Jews had so sanctified the Sabbath with rules that it was no longer a day set aside for Divine worship. Instead it became a day of stifling controls; a time when people, not adhering to the Sabbath Laws, would be hounded and penalized. Jesus admonished them: "The Sabbath was made for humankind and not humankind for the Sabbath" Mark 2:27. He declared that man was above the Sabbath and spurned their dictates on not helping the needy on the Sabbath. That he disdained petty observances, which they considered significant, roused their passions. They were being disregarded before their own people. Egos were hurt. And they would not take such an affront without retaliation.

THE LAW

At the age of six the Jew was inducted into the knowledge and practice of the law. By the time he was an adult, he was fully indoctrinated. Sin, guilt, atonement were impressed so deeply on his mind that God was seen as a Judge who summarily punished the offender, unless appeased through sacrifices. All activities were governed by the sacred books so much so the Prophet Mohammed of Islam called Judaism 'the religion of the book'. One such rule related to washing. The strict Jew had an obsessive fear of all kinds of pollution and had to be continually washing himself, as laid down in the law. That is why they faulted the apostles of Jesus who ate without washing their hands. Jesus responded typically: what goes into the mouth causes no offense; only malicious words that come out of it cause offense.

Time and again, Jesus showed by example that he not only respected the law but also urged others to respect the law

The Golden Rule

(Luke 17:14). He conformed to the ceremonial and judicial precepts of the old law. For example, when they asked for taxes he told Peter to pay the tax demanded (Matt 17:27). Despite his willingness to honor the law of the land and pay his taxes, they hoped to trap him on that very issue. "Then the Pharisees went and plotted to entrap him in what he said. So they sent their disciples to him, along with the Herodians, saying, 'Teacher, we know that you are sincere, and teach the way of God in accordance with truth, and show deference to no one; for you do not regard people with partiality .Tell us then, what do you think. Is it lawful to pay taxes to the Emperor, or not?' But Jesus, aware of their malice, said, 'Why are you putting me to the test, you hypocrites? Show me the coin used for the tax.' And they brought him a Denarius. Then he said to them, 'Whose head is this, and whose title?' They answered, 'The Emperor's.' Then he said to them, 'Give therefore to the Emperor the things that are the Emperor's, and to God, the things that are God's.' When they heard this, they were amazed; and they left him and went away" Matt 22:15-22. Aware of their malice and with caution, Jesus replied their questions which were fraught with implications. If he said 'do not pay' he could be reported to the

Emperor for rebellion. If he said 'pay', the people who were rebelling against Rome would find reason to distrust him. They thought he had no escape. He was trapped, back to the wall. They would watch him with glee, as he stood exposed. But Jesus was too much for them to handle. His pithy response had them running for cover. Smarting from defeat, they would wait to get even with him (Luke 11:53-54).

They feared that Jesus was out to demolish the law, incapacitate them, and take control. They felt threatened not just by his great knowledge, the authority with which he spoke, but more importantly by the response he got from the people. But for the people, what would they have not done? "Every day he was teaching in the Temple. The chief priests, the scribes, and the leaders of the people kept looking for a way to kill him; but they did not find anything they could do, for all the people were spell bound by what they heard" Luke 19:47-48

Despite their plots and threatening stance, Jesus allayed their fears when he reassured them that he had not come to abolish the Law but to fulfil it (Matt 5:17). The fulfillment was meant to come about by giving the law a humane interpretation; a new justice; a new way of life. "You have heard that it was said

The Golden Rule

to those of ancient times, 'You shall not murder'; and 'Whoever murders shall be liable to judgement.' But I say to you that if you are angry with a brother or sister, you will be liable to judgement" Matt 5:21-22. The new meaning was that hatred, which went before the murder needed therapy. Only then could the murder be stopped. By example he showed that hatred cannot replace hatred. He visited the homes of the Pharisees, who hated him, and supped with them in friendship. But Jesus did not hesitate to rebuke their hypocrisy (Mark 12:38). He faulted the deed, not the doer.

Unsuccessful in their efforts to do verbal duel with him they changed tack and decided to foist false witnesses on him (Mark 14:55-56). Even then they failed because the witnesses could not corroborate the statements they made. When they falsely accused him, his strong voice stayed silent. His silence was more eloquent than their vehement denunciation (Matt 27:12-14). Even Pilate who tried him was amazed at the way he conducted himself and sought to release him because he believed that Jesus was innocent.

The law in its mangled form was sprouting tentacles to reach out and encircle Jesus. Those growing tentacles closed in;

on Calvary, the place of his crucifixion.

POLITICAL INTRIGUE

In this law-governed, faction-ridden, male-dominated society, the political situation was typically cloak and dagger. Each group huddled in conspiracy to outwit the other. Vested interests defied the common good. Social climbers, religious pretenders, political heavyweights, used power and influence to have their way, as long as Rome was not ruffled.

THE ENVIRONMENT

In retrospect, what did the environment hold? A rather illiterate society, presided over by people in power who crafted outcomes in different situations to suit their interests. Structures in the groups were fairly well entrenched. The law was all embracing. Traditions and rituals were not questioned. Rome was in control, aided of course by scheming and self-seeking Jews. Not that all Jews were manipulators. Often the problem is in the system. If you put good people in a bad system, you will get bad results.

The hope of the Liberator, the Messiah, sustained many. But when he came, what a let-down it turned out to be! They

The Golden Rule

wanted revenge and the overthrow of the oppressor. He preached forgiveness and reconciliation. They feared the men in power who wanted to perpetuate the law, if nothing else, to hold sway over the masses. He exposed contradictions in the law and offered a new order; a radical change which was nothing short of unlocking the person trapped deep inside. The liberated person would be free of pretence, rid of double standards, shorn of duplicity, and far-removed from money-craze.

As a result of his new creed the groups were split down the middle into those who believed in him and those who refused to believe even what they saw. Against the might of the Roman Empire and the Jewish power brokers, what could 13 (Jesus and his twelve apostles) men do? How would Jesus manage his meager resources? How would he establish his new order? Did he stand a chance in this environment? His short life had all the answers.

Chapter 5
The Fully Human Professional

"Goodness in words creates trust, goodness in thinking creates depth; goodness in giving creates love."

~ Lao Tse

A certain company was going downhill. Morale was low and key personnel were leaving, afraid that things would get worse. The Chief Executive, who had taken over only a month ago, was disturbed at the drift in the value system of his top team. He decided to challenge his team to change. Ending an emotional address to them he said: "We are first and foremost human beings, then, either husbands or fathers or sons - and then we are professionals". He tried to remind them that professional priorities need not run counter to human values. That being a good professional was perfectly consistent with being a good person; rather, to be a good professional it was important to be a good person. With broad brush-strokes he painted a picture of the model each should follow so that the company operations, as a whole, would be the result of functions performed by enlightened professionals; of value-based actions. Jack Welch put it in different words: "Objectives and strategies don't get you there, values do". And pithy advice from Stephen R Covey makes sense: "For solutions during chaotic times, base it first on principles". Are they the values and principles that Jesus taught? There is good reason to believe that they are.

If one were to imagine Jesus in the place of that Chief Executive, addressing those professionals, would he have had anything different to say? Not likely. The message would have been much the same. But he would have stories to tell, embellished with figures of speech, and crisp conclusions. His words would hum like tuning forks and his listeners would be astounded. "We are first and foremost human beings," he would affirm. What would his words imply? That as humans we are part of a huge network, from which we cannot break free. Why? Since the fatherhood of God is a given, we must accept the brotherhood of humankind - a relationship that makes us unique. There are invisible cords that bind us; and those bonds get stronger with conscious help from within us.

Was Jesus part of this network? Did he have a stake in building relationships with the people of his time? Did he have to struggle like us? Shall we check the facts?

1) HUMAN

a) Human Traits: "He was a man like you and me," was how Kahlil Gibran referred to Jesus. As human beings we think, feel and express our needs. We like and dislike, love and hate, judge and misjudge, and experience pain and pleasure. It is the package that makes the person; not just one trait. Let us look for common qualities in Jesus and us. As a normal human being, he experienced hunger (Luke 4:2) and thirst (John 19:28) and therefore ate and drank (Matt 9:10). He felt tired (John 4:5) and slept (Luke 8:23). Jesus also expressed a wide range of human emotions. He was filled with joy (Luke 10:21), surprise (Mark 6:6), compassion (Luke 7:13) and disappointment (Luke 17:17). He embraced children (Mark 10:16) and empathized with suffering women (Luke 7:13). He wept for his friend Lazarus (John 11:35). He needed human company and support like any of us (Matt 26:38). But there were times when he wanted to be

The Golden Rule

left alone, even as we do (Matt 14:13). Sometimes he grew impatient with the foibles of his apostles and admonished them (Matt 17:17). In changed circumstances he changed his mind, as we do (John 7:8-10). When he found people hard-hearted and without mercy, he was angry (Mark 3:4-5). And became indignant when he saw the Temple desecrated, and drove out the money changers and those who were selling sacrificial animals (Matt 21:12-13). (In Jesus' day, activities at the Temple had taken on a commercial cast. Merchants sold sacrificial animals to pilgrims and foreigners at inflated prices. To visitors who paid in a different currency, money changers did not offer the correct rate of exchange and extracted an exorbitant fee. The system was designed more for profit than as an aid to worship, with a nexus between traders and the temple management. Justly indignant, Jesus responded by chasing out these defrauders. Then he turned his attention to those in real need.)

Was he afraid of rejection? Like any of us, he was, and John writes about it: "Because of this (teaching) many of his disciples (not the twelve) turned back and no longer went about with him. So Jesus asked the twelve, 'Do you also wish to go

Chapter 5 | The Fully Human Professional

away?'" John 6:66-67. The pathos in his words is palpable. Would the twelve reject him like the others? They were the closest and rejection by them would leave him friendless; he would feel abandoned if they left. But when those in his neighborhood and in his own town cold-shouldered him, he manfully coped with the affront, conceding that prophets do not find honor among their own and in their hometown (Mark 6:5). Knowing that different responses came from different segments, he wanted to know, how people really saw him (Matt 16:13). When the disciples told him that the general perception was that he was a prophet, he persisted (Matt 16:15), wanting to be told who they thought he was.

Towards the end of his public ministry, when suffering and death were imminent, he was deeply distressed and weighed down, recoiling at the very thought of excruciating pain and abject humiliation (Mark 14:13). He hoped to be comforted by his Apostles. The spirit was willing, not the flesh. They slept. And he felt forsaken.

Physically, he was very fit and strong. For several years he worked long hours as a carpenter, which gave him strong limbs and stamina. The punishment he took for many hours at the brutal hands of the Roman soldiers during his arrest and crucifixion was proof enough of his physical endurance. A lesser mortal would have collapsed and died before getting to Calvary, the hill where he was crucified.

The picture that emerges is of a person sharing with us flesh and blood, mind and memory, reason and emotion, likes and dislikes and normal human responses. He was born of an ordinary Jewish young woman, who descended from King David, though she had no pretensions to fame or wealth. He grew up in a small artisan's family, respecting social customs and religious practices of that time. He would have easily passed for the good kid across the street, because of his obedient conduct. When he came of age he learned a trade, as expected. Like a normal human, he grew in age and wisdom (Luke 2:52), which meant a stage-wise development as a man.

b) Intelligence: Even a cursory reading of the gospels gives us evidence of Jesus' intelligence. The speed with which he understood tricky questions put to him, the ready response he gave his adversaries, the ease with which he related to everyday human situations, the sharp comprehension he showed of puzzling matters, and his ability to read even the dark thoughts of those who challenged him (Matt 9:4), point to a well developed intelligence. He could separate fact from fiction, the relevant from the trivial and the momentous from the minor. In an intelligence quotient (IQ) test he would have scored remarkably well.

What of his emotional quotient (EQ)? Is that different from IQ? Emotional intelligence (as explained by Daniel Goleman), measured in terms of emotional quotient (EQ), is the ability to acquire and apply knowledge about one's emotions and the emotions of others, to ensure that problems are solved more successfully. Emotional intelligence is reflected in one's self-awareness, self-management, self-control, social awareness and social skills, all of which lead to the building of better relationships. It is about ways that influence others to give of their best. EQ gives one the advantage of reading non-verbal signals in facial and body movements and tone of voice; to understand what is said and what is not said. This skill is crucial, since studies show that 55% of communication is non-verbal. Despite these advantages, we tend to trust the information provided by the intellect more than vibes from emotion. Even the term 'emotional' does not appeal to reason, because it is viewed as a weak, out of control and childish response. The fact is different. EQ is more significant than IQ in successful people. Though some are academically brilliant, they are not as successful as they should be, because they lack the ability to socially interact and get the best out of others. They preen their own feathers and not stroke the feathers of others. With good reason the corporate world is shifting emphasis from IQ to EQ.

How did Jesus measure on the EQ scale? He was aware of his extraordinary talents and used them wisely. Not to flash them before admiring eyes, but only to succor the needy. He checked his impulses to retaliate; instead he forgave. He showed no temper tantrums; instead he remained unruffled under provocation. He was not rigid but flexible in his dealings with people. And of his social consciousness, his empathy, and willingness to get involved in the social problems of his time, examples are many. The Gospels record many situations where the non-verbal skills of the Master made the listener feel good. Jesus looked into the face of the person he was speaking with, touched those he healed, ate among the crowds, sat among them when the group was small, stood in their midst when the gathering was large and always adapted to the situation, not losing the common touch. His non-verbal messages gave his communication added meaning. Not only was his IQ high, but also his EQ outstanding. The combination was synergetic.

Danah Zohar and Ian Marshall, in their book, Connecting with our Spiritual Intelligence, assert that there is another important Q to consider – spiritual intelligence, expressed as spiritual quotient (SQ). Spiritual Intelligence, the authors explain, is the ultimate intelligence with which we address and solve problems of importance; the intelligence with which we can place our actions and our lives in a wider and meaningful context; the intelligence with which we can assess that one way of acting is better than another. In fact, the authors stress that SQ is the necessary foundation for both the IQ and EQ. They defend their thinking that ethical living and spirituality are not things of the past, but essential today. Can we question the SQ of Jesus, when almost the entire Gospels are a revelation of his spiritual intelligence?

As one who walked with his people, experienced what they experienced, suffered what they suffered, he knew from the inside, as it were, the possibilities and the limitations of being human. In his humanness, he resonated what is deepest

The Golden Rule

and best in us. And to confirm his humanness, he called himself 'The Son of Man'. Dorothy Sanders, summing up his human traits, writes in Christian Letters to a Post-Christian World: "He has himself gone through the whole human experience, from the trivial irritations of family life and the cramping restrictions of hard work, and the lack of money, to the worst horrors of pain and humiliation, defeat, despair and death".

As a human, he operated in very human situations. In those situations how did he manifest his beliefs and attitudes, knowledge, skills and work habits? Did he have skills of a high order? Did he have a style of his own? What was his profile? How different was it from those we know? We could begin by trying to understand what he considered as his goal; his mission.

2) MISSION

a) The Good News: In his words, proclaiming the good news, the new creed, the changed order, was important. That was his magnificent obsession. "I must proclaim the good news of the kingdom of God to the other cities also; for I was sent for this purpose" Luke 4:43.

What was the good news? It was the oxygen of life –

Love; love of God and love of fellowmen. Love is something we do; the giving of ourselves; the sacrifices we make, even for people who offend us, or do not love us in return. It is an act of will and not feeling, though feeling may accompany the act of will. Love is a value that is actualized through loving action. In a concrete way Jesus was both the message and the messenger.

What did he mean by 'the kingdom of God?' Mathew uses the term 30 times, Luke 31 times and Mark 14 times. Obviously it was a power-packed expression that conveyed more than the words literally meant. Some experts suggest that he referred to a liberated communion of subjects (in the kingdom), building transformed and lasting relationships; instead of bondage and alienation that is ordinarily seen in human affairs. His logic was simple: if we learn to love others, our relationships with them will improve. Ties with others will be redefined. And because of a new way of looking at our relationships we will feel empowered.

Since his mission was so vital he prepared himself through prayer, meditation and fasting (Matt 4:2), before he started preaching and teaching. Are we not reminded of how zealously and intensely we (humans like him) prepare when we undertake a major project?

b) Serving fellowmen: As an extension to proclaiming and teaching the good news, he had also come to serve his fellowmen (Luke 22:27). That was the second dimension to his mission, which he expressed lucidly, when he said: "You know that the rulers of the gentiles (non-Jews) laud it over them, and their great ones are tyrants over them. It will not be so among you; but whoever wishes to be great among you must be your servant, and whoever wishes to be first among you must be your slave; just as the Son of man came not to be served but to serve" Matt 20:25-28. By washing the feet of his Apostles, at the last supper before his death, he set a lasting example of what he meant by serving others.

c) Calling wrong-doers to repentance: The third dimension to his mission, was to call sinners to repentance – a goal that he articulates clearly to leave no one in doubt, "Jesus answered: Those who are well have no need of a physician, but those who are sick; I have come to call not the righteous but the sinners to repentance" Luke 5:31-32. And to explain the point, he asks a valid question, using a situation his listeners could relate to: "Which of you, having a hundred sheep and losing one of them, does not leave the ninety-nine in the wilderness and go after the one that is lost until he finds it? When he has found it, he lays it on his shoulders and rejoices" Luke 15:3-5. Going after the errant, to him, was serious business. In the parables of The Prodigal Son (Luke 15:11-32) and The Lost Coin (Luke 15:8-10) he reinforces this message.

LIVING HIS MISSION

How did he carry out his mission? By proclaiming the good news of love, serving his fellowmen and reaching out to sinners. Discern how one part flows into the next. If one had love of God and love of one's neighbor (the first part), serving one's neighbor would follow (the second part); and if one loved and served one's fellowman, one would be concerned over his drifting away and try to bring him back on course (the third part).The three parts mixed like waters; easily.

Against such a lofty mission how did Jesus perform?

a) The Gospels are packed with passages that recount his teachings on the Kingdom of God, the **good news.** The Gospels also narrate how he trained his apostles to carry on the good work. The crowds he attracted, the discourses he held, the

The Golden Rule

challenges he faced from his adversaries, which he converted into opportunities, all give ample evidence of his continuing attempts to put across the over-powering message of love: Love of God and love of one's neighbor. His frequent references to God and his eagerness to do His will put beyond any doubt his overwhelming love of God (John 14:31).

b) But what of his love for his fellowmen; how did he perform; did he **serve** his fellowmen as effectively as he declared? Here again the Gospels recount many situations when his compassion overflows. His empathy is seen in acts of succoring the needy – those who lived on the fringes of society. The emphasis here is not on his remarkable performance but on his willingness to help those in distress, not for acclaim or glory, but for love of his fellowmen.

c) What about **wrong doers**? They kept his company and he did not shun them (Matt 9:10). His unusual behavior was denounced by the Jewish Elders who condemned wrong-doers. Because Jesus did not follow their line, they tried to trap him. Consider the classic case: "The Scribes and the Pharisees brought a woman who had been caught in adultery: and making her stand before all of them, they said to him 'Teacher, this woman was caught in the very act of committing adultery. Now in the law, Moses commanded us to stone such a woman. Now what do you say?' They said this to test him, so that they might have some charge to bring against him. Jesus bent down and wrote with his finger. When they kept on questioning him, he straightened up and said to them, 'Let anyone among you who is without sin be the first to throw a stone at her.' And once again he bent down and wrote on the ground. When they heard it, they went away, one by one, beginning with the elders; and Jesus was left alone with the woman standing in front of him. Jesus straightened up and said to her, 'Woman, where are they? Has no one condemned you?' She said, 'No one, Sir.' And Jesus said 'Neither do I condemn you. Go your way, and from now on do not sin again'" John 8:3-11.

Perhaps, this encounter has no parallel in the Gospels for suspense and tension. Action swirls around Jesus, even as he stays calm. The Pharisees and the Scribes are waiting to pounce on him. The sinner herself has lost hope. Jesus remains unruffled, although the man involved in the adulterous act was not brought to him for justice, which was typical cover-up for the man, in a male-dominated society. It is after much

The Golden Rule

questioning that Jesus decides to speak. The woman's accusers are sure of snaring him. He has no escape, they think. The law is clear. The evidence is conclusive. He must condemn her. But what does he do? He does not act as Judge. He makes no accusation; he delivers no sermon; he only uses the law, which is their plank, to stand on. Only the sinless can condemn, he declares. Jewish law specifies that two innocent witnesses are to throw the first stones. 'Who among you is sinless', he implies, without pointing accusing fingers. In one deft stroke he demolishes their argument and exposes their hypocrisy. Tables are turned. The accusers become the accused. They know that he has seen through their dark motives. They move away stealthily and in disgrace. He bends down to write, so that they may flee unnoticed. They are vanquished. But there is no celebration. Only quiet reflection, as he bends down to write again. The woman expected no mercy from the crowds or from Jesus. She is surprised at the turn of events. Instead of condemnation, she receives forgiveness. Instead of punishment and death, she receives acquittal. What better way to illustrate his lesson? What better way to win her over to repentance? Later, he gently persuades the woman to change her sinful ways.

The Indian Poet, Thiruvalluvar, sang: "The best way to punish the wrong doer is to shame him/her by doing something good to him/her in return". Could there be greater good than calling him/her to repentance?

More examples could be cited from the Gospels, but the one we have just read is so overpowering that no other support is necessary.

A TREE IS KNOWN BY ITS FRUIT

What we see is that Jesus performed creditably in all three areas of his Mission. His own performance only reinforced his strong belief that performance mattered; for anyone, in any function. The slave in the parable he told, who did well by doubling the money entrusted to him was not only complimented but also suitably rewarded. "His master said to him: Well done, good and trustworthy slave: you have been trustworthy in a few things, I will put you in charge of many things; enter into the joy of your master" Matt 25:21. As expected, the non–performing slave in the same parable, who did not wisely use the money given to him, is reproached. Lucidly he summed up his thinking on non–performance when he said:

The Golden Rule

"Every tree that does not bear good fruit is cut down and thrown into the fire" Matt 7:19.

That his mission took up all of his waking hours, and that it gave his work a sense of urgency is made clear in Luke 12:50. Much was to be done. And there was so little time. His goal was to have his teaching reach the far corners of the world. He predicted that it would come to pass (Mark 14:9). His apostles saw to it. The Acts of the Apostles, the part that follows the four Gospels in the Bible, is a stirring account of how the apostles and their disciples set about spreading Jesus' message to different parts of the world.

3) BELIEFS

a) The Golden Rule: His strong beliefs gave his mission direction and momentum. At the top of the list of his beliefs is the Golden Rule: "In everything, do to others as you would have them do to you" Matt 7: 12. Put very simply, there is no room for double standards, which is following one rule for me and enforcing another for you. That is how we normally transact. No. That is not the way it should be, he entreats. Condensing many of his teachings, he declares that the Golden rule embodies the secrets of good relationships – value others as you value yourself. Over the centuries the world has agonized over this dictum. How can we treat others as we want to be treated? That is preposterous, the world argues. Self must precede others, it demands. That is why Law and Justice, distant cousins, are not on speaking terms. In delivering Justice, selfish variables intervene to distort a straight case that Law makes out. Translating Law into unbiased judgement is never easy when double standards will not give way. This shocking distortion was seen at Jesus' trial. Pilate was convinced that Jesus was innocent because his detractors could not prove their accusations. Law and Justice could have met on friendly terms, but for Pilate's strategy to play safe; to protect his interests. He did not want to be seen as offending the Roman Emperor, who would not tolerate a usurper. The Jews falsely accused Jesus of aspiring to become King. Pilate's selfishness and ambition put paid to Justice. He knew that he would face no problem in crucifying Jesus, because Jesus had no links with the Emperor. He did not value justice as much as he valued his position. Pilate failed the test. We, as professionals, also fail many times when we compromise the truth and put self over others and fair play.

The Golden Rule

The Golden Rule (Matt 7:12) is resented time and again because it calls us to rise above double standards, to disown foul play and to uphold fair play. Jesus' words test our sincerity, thoughts, words and deeds, because they nudge us to honor fair play; to give others what is due to them; to be unbiased and just. His words also apply to the choice we have to make between serving self and serving others. He does not suggest an exclusion of self, but an inclusive behavior which embraces others as well. We recall that he advocates love for others as strongly as he encourages love of ourselves. It follows that love for self is not against his teachings, but a part of it. With God, as the Father, whom we love, others and we are bonded inseparably.

It is true that some other great thinkers also spoke and wrote of the Golden Rule, in different words (Example, the Jewish Talmud: "What is hurtful to yourself, do not do to your fellowmen"). Why then does Jesus' teaching on the Golden Rule stand out? For two reasons: One, Jesus spoke with authority; the others offered a suggestion that they painstakingly tried to formulate into a teaching. They were men with feet of clay – they erred, like many of us. In sharp contrast, there was no dichotomy in the way Jesus spoke and acted – upholding the truth in all circumstances. Even his critics and adversaries could not accuse Jesus of wrong doing. He was blameless. That is why his character towers over the others who also proposed the Golden Rule.

Two, Jesus does not negatively express the Rule, as some others do. (For example: "What you do not want done to yourself, do not do to others". Confucius). It is easier to avoid doing evil to others, than to take the initiative and do good. The Golden Rule, as Jesus taught it, is the foundation of active goodness and mercy. It is fundamental to building good relationships.

b) One cannot serve two masters: He vividly stated another of his beliefs: "No slave can serve two masters; for a slave will either hate the one and love the other, or be devoted to the one and despise the other" Luke 16: 13. We cannot choose good and evil at the same time. We must be careful in the hard choices we make, he avers. These choices might not be related to persons (masters), but deities that we install and worship; anything to which we get enslaved. For example, one cannot go after Fame and Modesty (two very different masters), at the same time. That would be a contradiction. The pursuit of fame tends to make one, in the words of St. Paul, 'puffed up'. Jesus implies that we would have to reconcile our goals in life to bring some order into our confused minds and set our priorities right. When our priorities are not right, we give the less important ones more attention and the more important ones less of it; that is when results are far from satisfactory.

c) To be wise: In our transactions with others, Jesus does not condone naivety and foolishness. In a parable of practical dimensions, he tells of five prudent virgins who pour enough oil in their lamps and of five naive and foolish virgins who do not fill their lamps with enough oil, to join the bridegroom's procession with lighted lamps. When the bridegroom arrives, the wise virgins join the procession and attend the banquet (a practice that was popular at that time), but the foolish ones are shut out (Matt. 25:1-13). Foolish behavior has no excuse. Without reserve, he commends the wise (Matt 10:16) and advocates alertness and foresight (Luke 12:35). Such wisdom, he says, will surely find expression in shrewd common sense. He cites two situations to make the point: "For which of you, intending to build a tower does not first sit down and estimate the cost to see whether he had enough to complete it?" Luke 14: 28. And, "what king, going out to wage war against another king, will not sit down first and consider whether he is able with ten thousand to oppose the one who comes against him with twenty thousand?" Luke 14: 31. Shrewd Commonsense is the canopy that stretches across all his teachings and actions. Holding up the canopy of commonsense are two stalwarts - **Honesty and Fidelity,** whom he exalts when he says: "Whoever is faithful in a very little is faithful also in much; and whoever is dishonest in a very little is dishonest also in much" Luke 16: 10. Honesty and fidelity are not minor but major virtues, he stresses. And having them makes sense when transacting with others, because we compromise relationships without them.

d) Attachment to wealth: Does honesty have a bearing on a man's attitude to material possessions, to wealth? Is an unbecoming attachment to material acquisitions approved? Jesus has very definite ideas on such attachment (Luke 12:23). In a world that is wealth-starved, his words are not food for such hunger. "And he said to them: Take care! Be on your guard against all kinds of greed; for one's life does not consist in the abundance of possessions" Luke 12: 15. It cannot be denied that greed tests honesty; and that avarice leads to compromise. To prove the point that he made no exceptions, speaking of himself, he said that he had nowhere to lay his head. He had no place to call his home (Matt 8:20). He had no possessions to call his own; and no money. Greed and avarice had not got the better of him. But he is practical. He is not against money. Money has its use. It is necessary. What he is against is an obsessive attachment to money because it warps values. St. Paul conveyed the Master's thinking lucidly: "For the love of money is the root of all kinds of evil" 1 Timothy 6:10. Money is not the root of all evil, but the excessive love of money.

S. K. Chakraborty and Pradip Bhattacharya, in their book, Human Values - The Tagorean Panorama, explain briefly why attachment to wealth is obstructive: "Christ had said, just as it is impossible for a camel to pass through the eye of a needle, so it is impossible for a rich man to attain salvation. The meaning is:---- he, too, because of his increasing grossness (attachments), cannot make his way into the universal".

In a parable, Jesus puts things in perspective: "A man planted a vineyard, and leased it to tenants, and went to another country for a long time. When the season came, he sent a slave to the tenants in order that they might give him his share of the produce of the vineyard" Luke 20:9-10. We have a right to our share of the produce; to our share of profit. No one can take away that right. Profit is not a dirty word. Money is not obscene. Work must be rewarded. In the case of the laborer, he is very specific: "For laborers deserve their food," Matt 10:10, and their wages too.

Stephen R Covey echoes these statements when he exhorts us to make money for noble reasons; for the family, for example. But he advises against money becoming the center. Such attachment, he warns, could bring about one's undoing. Covey adds, that with money, at best, we could buy people's hands and backs, but not their hearts and brains; not their loyalty and creativity.

e) Responding to enemies: When we are not attached to wealth or possessions and fair to others, we believe that there will be no discord. But fair conduct does not insulate us from all dangers. Enemies sprout, almost from nowhere, through jealousy, sadism, or sheer cussedness. How are we to handle such enemies? "I say to you, love your enemies." Matt 5: 44. The advice Jesus gives is difficult to follow. Almost impossible,

The Golden Rule

we may contend. Jesus takes it further: "But if anyone strikes you on the right cheek, turn the other also" Matt 5: 39.

Jesus' words, in today's context, have bothered many people. We can understand them better when we remember that the custom in Jesus' day was to give a light left-handed slap on the face of an adversary to show disdain for him. This was not meant to be a painful blow, but an insult. Jesus must have startled his listeners when he suggested offering the other cheek also. He was not suggesting that force must never be used to restrain evil. Rather, he was saying that by offering the other cheek we reject the spirit of retaliation towards those who offend us, and we offer them forgiveness.

There are some critics who insist that he should have practiced what he preached when the soldier struck him after his arrest. Why did he not turn the other cheek? Instead he questions the soldier (John 18:23). There is a contradiction, they conclude. Again, he questions the crowd who want to stone him (John 10:31-32). Here too, the critics are emphatic that there is a contradiction. To resolve these contradictions, we shall have to go back to the Golden Rule (Matt 7:12). What he meant was: Love your neighbor as much as you love yourself. Love of self is

Chapter 5 | The Fully Human Professional

important. It is not taboo. Only if we love ourselves, can we love our neighbor. We cannot let the Self be exploited or abused, without protest. Jesus showed by prudent action that one has a right to love and protect oneself. "So from that day on they planned to put him to death. Jesus therefore no longer walked about openly among the Jews, but went from there to a town called Ephraim in the region near the wilderness; and he remained there with his disciples" John 11:53-54. By staying clear of his enemies, he showed no bravado; just sensible behavior. If protecting oneself is important and right, Jesus did no wrong in defending himself against unjust soldiers or a frenzied mob. There was another compelling reason: He had yet to complete his mission. More work had to be done. His time for Calvary had not yet come.

His maxim on the enemy must be seen in the context of the Jewish law which stated: "An eye for an eye and a tooth for a tooth" Matt 5:38. That was the law. Retaliate. Give back in equal measure. Against that conditioning to persuade the Jews to think differently was difficult. Jesus spoke of love and not retaliation. He was emphatic on forgiving offenders and not nursing grudges against them. But he was also for confronting injustice; for protesting violence. Therefore, his questioning the soldiers and the crowd was not retaliation, but the questioning of injustice. Standing up for what was just, non-violently. As a human he had his rights and stood up for them. Later, at the time of his arrest Peter brandished a sword and cut off the ear of a soldier. Jesus admonished him (Matt 26:52). He would not condone tit-for-tat behavior from Peter, his apostle. Still later, at his passion he endured abject humiliation without a question. His silence amazed his persecutors. He knew that he could not reason with them, since their minds were warped. Pilate also knew that the Chief Priests handed over Jesus out of jealousy and not because he was guilty of wrong-doing (Mark 15:10).

f) Truth: Pilate was intrigued at the way Jesus conducted himself during the trial. When Jesus said that he had come to testify to the truth, Pilate asks a rhetorical question: "What is truth?" John 18:38. Pilate does not ask: 'What is the truth?' Jesus did not answer the Governor because there was no room for words when he stood as testimony to truth. On an earlier occasion he called himself the truth. Truth in Greek philosophy is what is opposed to falsehood. In Hebrew thinking, Truth is more definite, suggestive of trustworthiness, steadfast love.

That personified Jesus – steadfast love in upholding and living the truth, in word and deed. And that is why he affirmed that the truth sets one free, while the opposite binds one in knots.

It does take some intent and effort to understand and resolve the apparent contradiction between his exhortation and example. In the end Jesus stands vindicated. He showed no double standards. He lived his beliefs. Like reflections from a diamond that cannot be separated from the source, his beliefs were part of his enlightened Mission; inseparable.

4) KNOWLEDGE

The Gospels extol his superior knowledge of the Scriptures (The Old Testament) from where he quoted frequently. He discussed with scribes and Pharisees and engaged them in animated debate. He resolved doubts raised even by those in high positions. Even the Scribes who were the acclaimed experts, the doctors of the Law, were amazed at his understanding and his answers (Luke 2:47). His knowledge was never in doubt: "They were astounded by his teaching, for he taught them as one having authority, and not as the scribes" Mark 1:22. The crowds who heard him comprised the low, middle, and upper classes. Most of them were tutored in the Jewish Law and were acquainted with the Old Testament. So for them to be 'astounded' was making a statement on his knowledge and ability to communicate that knowledge.

To explain his teachings, Jesus referred to the work experience of builders, soldiers, doctors, teachers, tax collectors, farmers, traders, business managers, land owners, fisher folk, shepherds and loan sharks. He was familiar with the ploughing of fields, sowing of seeds, harvesting, winnowing crops and storing produce in barns. He knew the relative merits of soil and their impact on crop yield. He talked on the vagaries of weather. He spoke of the need to dispose of weeds wisely and to prune vines to increase fruitfulness. He spoke of birds, trees, other vegetation, fish, insects, serpents and animals. His personal experience as a carpenter gave him first-hand knowledge of timber, furniture and the building industry. He knew the joys and customs of happy occasions like weddings; and the sorrows of sad occasions like death and funerals. He was aware of problems that families faced; the plight of the marginalized; the hazards of life from the actions of lawless people and the injustice that the rich could unleash. People even approached him to resolve legal disputes.

TOTAL QUALITY MANAGEMENT

The passage that follows was gleaned from several available: "Then Jesus said to the disciples: There was a rich man who had a manager, and charges were brought to him that this man was squandering his property. So he summoned him and said to him, 'What is this that I hear about you? Give me an accounting of your management, because you cannot be my manager any longer" Luke 16:1-2. Notice the terms Jesus uses: 'Manager, Management, Accounting'; everyday language in corporate circles. Note also his emphasis on proper management where the manager is held accountable.

In business circles there has been much talk on Total Quality Management – TQM. We could hazard a guess that TQM found favor with Jesus 2000 years ago. How? In simple terms TQM is a way of transacting that helps the Company to meet Customer expectations and to continually improve on the quality of such transactions. This implies Customer focus. It means finding out what the Customer expects and orienting the Company to deliver just that; perhaps more; and to make profit

The Golden Rule

in the process. So 'listen to the customer and respond' would be the axiom.

Let us examine how Jesus went about listening and responding to his customers. Virtually everyone who came to him got a prompt response; with no condescension; only empathy. Their expectations were exceeded. They were delighted. Even his adversaries (the Scribes) had to grudgingly admit to their satisfaction, as Luke 20:39 points out: "Then some of the scribes answered: 'Teacher, you have spoken well'". And John 7:45-46 refers to yet another compliment: "Then the temple police went back to the Chief Priests and the Pharisees, who asked them: 'Why did you not arrest him?' The police answered: 'Never has anyone spoken like this'". With Oliver Goldsmith we could recite: "those who came to scoff remained to pray". So forceful and complete was his response to his customers that in despair, the Pharisees then said to one another: "You see you can do nothing. Look the world has gone after him!" John 12:19. The competition was definitely worried. The CSI (Customer Satisfaction Index), if there was a way of measuring it then, would have been a chart-buster and a trend-setter.

Chapter 5 | The Fully Human Professional

The TQM concept extends to the internal Customer – the employees. Their satisfaction mattered. The assumption being, that only a satisfied employee would try to satisfy the company's customers. If the apostles are regarded as employees (subordinates), their statements and actions would give us an idea of the Employee Satisfaction Index (ESI).

When Jesus enquired if the twelve apostles would forsake him like some other disciples who refused to walk with him, Simon Peter, speaking for the team, said: "Lord, to whom can we go?" John 6: 68. They excluded all options. They were with him. That would not change.

Perhaps the spontaneous tribute that Thomas, the apostle, paid Jesus is unsurpassed: "Let us also go, that we may die with him" John 11:16. And Peter's unreserved declaration adds credibility to Thomas' idea of solidarity with the Master: "I will lay down my life for you" John 13: 37. Jesus identified himself with his apostles, his team. In return they gave him a massive mandate.

TQM also implies continuous improvement. In his ministry, Jesus set about continually improving the disposition

The Golden Rule

of people. That is why some call him a Change Agent. Peter, the fisherman, turned apostle, denied Jesus three times; only to later lay down his life for him. Mathew, the tax collector, gave up his money craze, to become his apostle and stay faithful to his calling. Zacchaeus, the chief tax collector, who defrauded people, promised to make good four-fold to those he cheated, after his encounter with Jesus. The woman caught in adultery, found forgiveness and acquittal. She would not have profited from the Jewish Law in the same way. The Samaritan woman at the well, who, at different times had lived with five men, had a change of heart and invited the people of the town to meet Jesus and listen to his teachings. The Centurion, shedding his Roman ways, told Jesus that only a word from him would be enough to heal his servant. Nicodemus, a highly placed Pharisee, went to Jesus to unlearn and learn. The crucified thief on his right, at Calvary, begged Jesus to remember him and rebuked his unrepentant fellow thief, who was hanging to the left of Jesus. Just a few names are put down here. In each case, Jesus brought about a transformation, as a change agent who redefined values and relationships. He showed them, very subtly, that the conflict in them sprang from greed, lust, hatred and attachment. He showed them how, kindness, compassion, honesty, respect and generosity, would make a big difference; how change was just a decision away.

The sign of a good Change Agent or Change Leader is the habit of abandoning yesterday and embracing today and tomorrow. Peter Drucker called this 'organized abandonment'. Jesus did not dwell on the past. He placed before each person the present and the future: 'Go and do likewise and Go and sin no more'. It was always the future; never the past. He did not ask them: "Why did you sin yesterday?" or "Why did you behave badly yesterday?"

TQM aims at profit from improved performance. So if TQM found favor with Jesus, the question that follows is: What profit did Jesus earn? Jesus kept no accounts. To him the profit was the changed attitude, the reformed disposition, the new mindset of those he tried to transform. When that happened, he profited; and going by the many that changed, Jesus profited immensely. The bottom line looked healthy. And if his company stocks were traded, the market would have turned bullish.

Edward Juran and Joseph Demming initiated and

propagated quality concepts, culminating in TQM. Without taking credit away from them, we must assert that Jesus operated on the same lines without giving the process a name. With his listeners we may exclaim: "How does this man have such learning!" John 7: 15.

5) SKILLS

Now, let us consider the skills that Jesus demonstrated. People were 'amazed' at his range of skills. His Team management skills, interpersonal skills, communication skills made a great impact on people of that time. These skills call for separate and special treatment, and therefore appear under separate chapters. Lessons for professionals will be drawn in these chapters.

6) WORK HABITS

He was not content camping at one place, waiting for his Customers to come to him. Instead he went out to them and worked long hours at his Mission, as Luke writes: "Soon afterwards he went on through cities and villages, proclaiming and bringing the good news of the kingdom of God" Luke 8:1. He had only three years of public ministry, and had to make the best use of each day. So he began early, as Mark 1:35 points out: "In the morning, while it was still very dark, he got up and went out". And like all good leaders, he cultivated an eye for detail, even when planning his itinerary, as Mark 3:9 states: "He told his disciples to have a boat ready for him because of the crowd, so that they do not crush him". Good professionals learn to use available resources effectively; not deriding paltry ones. On more than one occasion we see him use his resources prudently, often improvising and advising his apostles to do likewise.

As a **professional** his **mission, beliefs, knowledge, skills and work habits** fuse, to uncover a **human** of rare excellence. This outstanding professional walks, so to speak, like a colossus, leaving giant footprints.

The Golden Rule

Chapter 6

Relationship with the Team

"We are all angels with one wing; we can fly while embracing each other."

~ *Luciano de Crescenzo*

Some people steal credit from their team-mates to appear bigger than they are. They hog the limelight, belittling the contributions of their team fellows. 'Tragic' is a word that comes to mind when referring to such sorry specimens. Little do they realize that leaders cannot complete projects without the help of teams! That even a grand scheme is crippled without the right team. Therefore, a professional with foresight selects team members that can help him achieve team objectives. To get the best out of them, he nurtures them, values each in the group and assigns credit to each for contributions made.

In his essay, The Twelve Men, dealing with the British

The Golden Rule

Jury system, G.K. Chesterton wrote: "Whenever our civilization wants a library to be catalogued, or a solar system discovered, or any other trifle of this kind, it uses up its specialists. But when it wishes anything done, which is really serious, it collects twelve of the ordinary men standing around. The same thing was done, if I remember right, by the founder of Christianity".

Jesus Christ was into something serious. To spread messages born of his mission, he needed a team to assist him. For that he chose twelve ordinary men, who were known as the apostles. These twelve were given a mammoth task: 'To be the light of the world and the salt of the earth'. Very ambitious tasks, by their standards. Jesus did not stop at that. He raised the bar even higher, exhorting them to: "Be perfect" Matt 5: 48. That was the ultimate. He knew, even as he set those standards, that they were frail, very ordinary men. Attaining high standards would be almost impossible for them. Yet, to Jesus what mattered was the effort. The Japanese have a nice way of saying it: fall down seven times, but get up eight. Jesus conveyed, exactly that to his team. Do not give up trying.

What were the names of the twelve Apostles? "These are the names of the twelve Apostles; first, Simon, also known as

Chapter 6 | Relationship with the Team

Peter, and his brother Andrew; James son of Zebedee, and his brother John; Philip and Bartholomew; Thomas and Mathew the tax collector; James Son of Alphaeus, and Thaddaeus; Simon the Cananaean, and Judas Iscariot, the one who betrayed him" Matt 10: 2-4.

Most of the apostles do not have detailed character descriptions in the Gospels. From the sketchy references of them, we find that Peter was spontaneous and impulsive. He often spoke for the rest, in a way demonstrating his leadership quality. John, also known as the Beloved apostle, was comparatively young and given to passionate outbursts. With his brother James, he jockeyed for the best positions. Mathew, the tax collector, was better educated, but despised because of the job he once held. Simon (the Cananaean) was a Zealot - the group given to violence and rioting. Andrew was sociable and open. His Greek friends are referred to in the Gospels. He is seen as one willing to help his friend Philip and one who operates at his own pace. Philip is described as pure in spirit, simple and not given to manipulating others; and rather shy. Jesus warmly compliments Bartholomew (Nathaniel) as one who has no deceit in him. Trifle impetuous and generous to a fault, is Thomas; often referred to as 'Doubting

The Golden Rule

Thomas', because he refused to believe that Jesus had risen from the dead. The Gospels are rather silent on James, son of Alphaeus and Thaddaeus. Judas (like Jesus) was a common name for Jewish men in those days. It is the Greek form of Judah. He came from a region called Judea; the other apostles came from Galilee. Yet Judas Iscariot gained enough trust to be given the position of Treasurer of the team. He had political aspirations and hoped that Jesus would help fulfil them. We are not sure, but some experts put down his betrayal of Jesus to disillusionment. His leader would not occupy high positions. How then could he? What fanned his hopes for a time was the attempt by the people to force Jesus to become king. Not he alone, but the others also were impressed each time Jesus was acclaimed by the crowds. They expected that such ovation would build to a crescendo which would have political overtones. But that was not to be. The Master did not seek public office. He had different objectives.

a) Choosing his team: How did Jesus go about choosing these men? The fact remained that he chose them (John 6:70). The brief account of their selection is fascinating. In a head hunting exercise he planted a seed in them. They let the seed germinate: "As he walked by the sea of Galilee, he saw two brothers, Simon, who is called Peter, and Andrew his brother, casting a net into the sea - for they were fishermen. And he said to them, 'Follow me, and I will make you fish for people.' Immediately they left their nets and followed him. As he went from there, he saw two other brothers, James son of Zebedee and his brother John, in the boat with their father Zebedee, mending their nets, and he called them. Immediately they left the boat and their father, and followed him" Matt 4:18-22. We also read of his team selection in John 1:43. We cannot help admiring the charisma of the man who called them to give up their all and follow him; almost in an act of total surrender. They showed no hesitation, only immediate compliance. They were prepared to break with their past and not stop to enquire what the change would give them in return. They did not check on the kind of hardships they would have to endure. He called. That was all that mattered (Luke 5:11). It may be argued that they had very little to give up. True. But it must not be forgotten that the little they had was all that they had - their livelihood and their families.

Why did Jesus choose such men; such a motley crowd? Why not others with better profiles? We do not have definite answers. But some assumptions are possible. Perhaps he found it easier to train and mold these simple people, rather than the I-know-it-all type. The twelve were prepared to unlearn and learn again. Another assumption is that Jesus had very little option. Most common people were illiterate. Of course, in the Gospels we meet people in high positions. But they seem to have their attachments: to money, to possessions, to positions. They were not the right type to join a leader who moved from village to village, town to town, gypsy-like.

b) Structure: Of the twelve, Simon Peter is first. Mathew makes that clear. Peter's name is repeated 195 times in the gospels. Together, all the others find their names included 130 times. From the beginning Peter was chosen to lead the rest. With him as the key figure, Jesus sought to establish an Inner Circle, a core group. Peter, James and John made up this next-to-Jesus-level (Mark 9:12). The other nine came next. He began with twelve, but had to expand the size of the team, as the scale of operations widened. He appointed another seventy (Luke 10:1). In corporate parlance one could say that Jesus set up a flat structure. Twelve on the one side subtly separated into the inner circle of three, and the remaining nine. On the other side were the more recently recruited group of 70. Although he dealt with the two groups directly, one might assume that the new group of 70 sought the help of the 12 in transacting with the Master. A dotted line relationship is visualized. Although some others wished to join him, he was not eager to enlist more disciples into his team.

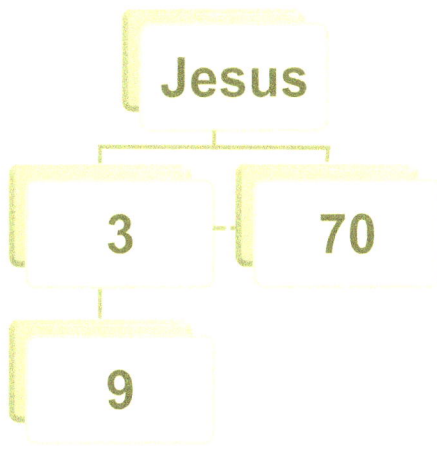

c) Managing a weak team: His team was as frail and disjointed as those we have in corporate circles today. They were ambitious and squabbled over favored positions (Luke 9:46). Even at the emotional last supper, they worried about rank and status. Despite Jesus' assurances (Matt 10:31), meant to dispel fear, they were a timid lot, anxious and stressed; who deserted him and fled when the Roman soldiers arrested him (Matt 26:56). They amply demonstrated the mixture of good and bad qualities present in

The Golden Rule

most of us. Yet, unlike most of us they were dense. With them some of the most obvious facts did not register; they understood little (Luke 18:34). Therefore Jesus had to contend not just with their human infirmities, but also with their low level of understanding, making his task all the more difficult. But like a good big brother (although he was younger than most of them) he took them into his huge embrace - warts and all - and called them his friends: "I do not call you servants any longer, because the servant does not know what the master is doing; but I have called you friends, because I have made known to you everything" John 15:50

d) Expecting obedience and commitment: What made up for their obvious weakness was their willingness to abide by the conditions, Jesus laid down: "If any want to become my followers, let them deny themselves and take up their cross and follow me" Matt 16:24. Total commitment was the entrance fee to this exclusive club. And they willingly paid that fee. A sign of such commitment was obedience. Knowing that Jesus valued their obedience, they readily complied (Matt 21:6). These faithful followers were always close to him. He spent most of the three years of his public ministry in their company as he grew to love them and treat them with great affection. They responded not out of duty, but because they loved him. No man had ever struck such a responsive cord in their hearts. He had stirred in them a dormant capacity to love, that even his commands were received through doors of love. St. Paul wrote of such a relationship in one of his letters: "For this reason, though I am bold enough in Christ to command you to do your duty, yet I would rather appeal to you on the basis of love" Paul to Philemon Vs 8-9. Much, much later, Dag Hammarskjold, former UN Secretary General, echoed the same thought: "Your position never gives you the right to command. It only imposes on you the duty of so living your life that others can receive your order without being humiliated".

Although the apostles were slow to understand, they were the privileged ones, because they had Jesus with them ready to explain his teachings to them (Luke 8:10). The process of teaching them was long and arduous since they were slow to understand. But he did not relent; they had to pass from apprenticeship to discipleship; which they eventually did. When they had gained some insights, he knew it was time to give them a task: "And he sent them out to proclaim the Kingdom of God" Luke 9: 2

e) Springing to their defense: Since he had a weak team

he had to jealously watch over them. Notice how he leaps to their defense when the Pharisees fault them: "At that time Jesus went through the grain fields on the Sabbath; his disciples were hungry, and they began to pluck heads of grain to eat. When the Pharisees saw it, they said to him, 'Look, your disciples are doing what is not lawful to do on the Sabbath'. He said to them, 'Have you not read what David did when he and his companions were hungry? He entered the house of God and ate the bread of the Presence, which is not lawful for him or his companions to eat, but only for the priests'" Matt 12:1-4. King David was among the more respected figures in the Old Testament. His example silenced the accusers; if he could eat the bread kept in the house of God, then the disciples of Jesus could eat grain plucked from the field. Using Scripture (The Old Testament), the very weapon they used to inflict hurt on his apostles, he parried every thrust. With their weapon blunted, they saw no point in a sustained attack on the apostles. They retreated. This was just a war of words. Watch what he does when physical danger threatens his apostles. He throws himself between the soldiers and the apostles: "So if you are looking for me, let these men go" John 18:8.

f) Adopting different approaches: Knowing that each was

different, he adopted different approaches. Different strokes for different folk, one might explain. Let us look at some of those approaches. First, the disciples of John the Baptist, Andrew and John, wanted to join Jesus. But they were timid and withdrawn. He does not wait for them to make the first move. He takes the initiative and speaks with them. Then they wish to know where he stays. He promptly invites them over, and puts them at ease. Second, with Peter it is different. Peter has no inhibitions; open and ready. Jesus spots the potential in him and entrusts him with the responsibility of leading the rest. He wins warm praise; also strong rebuke when he strays. Gaining maturity is a process which takes time. It calls for patience and perseverance from the mentor. Peter was transformed through this maturing process, overseen by the Master. The firebrand Peter we see in the early chapters of the Gospels and the mellowed Peter we encounter in The Acts of the Apostles (a later part of the New Testament) confirm this transformation. Peter had matured and the Master's touch was all too visible. Third, Philip followed when he was asked to follow. But he needed clarification. Jesus spends time with him, keeping him enthralled in a long conversation. Fourth, Jesus praises Bartholomew (Nathaniel), and the one without guile loves it. As seen in the four situations, Jesus used different methods in tutoring his apostles to gain their confidence.

Jesus got to the heart of his people and to the heart of the subject with a very simple and personal approach. Friendly, trusting and encouraging, he adapted to the needs of each – treating each in a special way. He was not distant or superior; rather, close and accessible. How did he do that? By being with them constantly and demonstrating to them how his words could be translated into deeds; by interpreting his parables and teachings for them; and by uniting them into a cohesive team. Although he had crowds around him for most of the time, he concentrated on training his apostles. He would have to leave them behind. And they would have to be ready; each dealt with differently.

g) Permitting freedom, not licence: Such interactions with the Master gave them a sense of freedom. They could discuss his teachings with him freely; get doubts clarified - many times, if necessary (Mark 10:10). As some one rightly wrote, "Doubt is one foot lifted, poised to step forward or backward. There is no motion until the foot comes down". When doubts lead to questions, and questions lead to answers, and the answers are accepted, then doubts have done a good job – the foot has come down with a purpose. In a typical discussion, Peter puts it bluntly to the Lord: What can we expect? The answer that Jesus gives him is not only complete, but more importantly, unalloyed motivation: "Peter began to say to him, 'Look, we have left everything and followed you.' Jesus said, 'Truly I tell you, there is no one who has left house or brothers or sisters or mother or father or children or fields, for my sake and for the sake of the good news who will not receive a hundredfold'" Mark 10: 28-30. Such freedom of seeking clarification did not mean license. When they had to be chided, he did it without hesitation. Peter was questioned when he showed little faith (Matt 14:31) and the team was reprimanded (Mark 8:17) when their behavior baffled him. Very shrewdly he tested them (John 6:5-6) from time to time, cautioned them to be discreet (Luke 9:36), alert (Matt 24:50) and warned them against setting bad examples (Luke 17:1). Despite their closeness there were times when he had to over-rule them; this he did without flinching (Luke 18:15-16). Very rightly he maintained a healthy distance, not letting the relationship be taken for granted. There was respect, almost awe for the Master. With his apostles he showed that a fine balance had to be kept between freedom and discipline. One without the other would be counter-productive, as Cullen Hightower stresses: "Discipline without freedom is tyranny. Freedom without discipline is chaos".

h) Showing understanding: His sternness gave way to magnanimity and deep understanding when a defaulting apostle repented. Peter denied Jesus; but repented and wept bitterly. Not once did Jesus remind him of his denial. There was no reproach even in his tone. No change in his love for Peter. No demotion from the leadership position he had given Peter. On the contrary, Jesus confirms Peter's appointment as the leader (John 21:16). Peter would be his successor and that would not change. Judas was not repentant. But Jesus shows no hostility; only understanding. When he brings soldiers to arrest him, he says: "Friend, do what you are here to do" Matt 26:50. Jesus asks his apostles to stay awake and pray with him, as they await the traitor. Instead they fall asleep. Even at that critical hour, before his arrest, Jesus shows patience. He does not chastise them; there is only pain in his voice and sadness on his face.

i) Leading by example: Before beginning an intimate meal with his disciples, the Last Supper, Jesus gave them a lesson in humility. Normally, slaves performed the act of washing the feet of dinner guests. Here Jesus, the guest of honor, dressed himself like a slave, with a towel around his waist and insisted on washing the feet of his disciples. By doing that, he gave them a lasting example in humbly serving others: "After he had washed their feet, had put on his robe, and had returned to the table, he said to them, 'Do you know what I have done to you? You call me Teacher and lord - and you are right, for that is what I am. So if I, your Lord and Teacher, have washed your feet, you also ought to wash one another's feet; for I have set you an example that you also should do as I have done to you'" John 13: 12-15.

j) Identifying with them: So closely did he relate to the apostles that he identified himself with them, emphasizing: "Whoever welcomes you, welcomes me" Matt 10: 40. Luke puts the same thought in different words: "Whoever listens to you listens to me, and whoever rejects you, rejects me" Luke 10:16

Perhaps the greatest tribute the apostles paid Jesus is found in John's Gospel: "And his disciples believed in him" John 2: 11. The statement is rather simplistic. But it uncovers the pinnacle of faith they had climbed. When the learned Pharisees and Scribes proudly refused to accept Jesus, despite his great teachings and mighty works, most of which were foretold in the

The Golden Rule

Scriptures, these simple people rallied round him. He returned their compliment fittingly: "You are those who stood by me in my trials" Luke 22: 28.

k) Delegating: In time, and with training, the apostles were being groomed for higher responsibility. The time for delegation was at hand; true delegation with authority. Jesus did this about two years into his public ministry. Sooner would have been catastrophic; later would have been too late. His timing was near perfect. He had selected simple folk like James and Andrew to represent him to the world. And to them he gave his own authority and power. First, he sent out the twelve, and later the seventy new recruits (Mark 6:7). Delegation, empowerment according to some, is the willingness to let go. It is the willingness to let others make mistakes. It is the willingness to trust team-fellows. And it is the willingness to establish and use broad controls. Jesus followed these norms faithfully. His example would inspire his apostles to adopt similar measures later. On their first assignment he gave them broad guidelines to follow. When they returned they reported to him (Mark 6:30) and (Luke 10:17). The joyful reporting symbolized a fulfillment of the task assigned to them. Even in those days, Jesus ensured that they gained job satisfaction.

Jesus also knew that his team needed to take a break from the punishing schedule they followed. Soul and body needed rest, which he gave them (Mark 6:31).

Jesus knew that his life was short and his public ministry, a brief three years. His apostles had to be readied to carry on the task, of fulfilling the Mission - of reaching his message to the ends of the earth. He could not tarry. He had to move on. The need to move on is explained with the right metaphor in the Biography of Vivekananda: "How often does a man ruin his disciples by remaining always with them? When men are trained, it is essential that their leader leave them, for without his absence they cannot develop themselves. Plants always remain small under a big tree". (Advvaita Ashrama Mayavati)

I) Ensuring succession: We shall have to return to Peter, because he played a decisive role in managing the team, despite his many weaknesses. After the Master's death they were distraught and looked for some consolation in their old occupation – fishing. "Simon Peter said to them, 'I am going fishing.' They said to him, 'we will go with you'" John 21: 3. Note the difference. They do not say, 'we too will go fishing', but say, 'we will go with you', to signify that they would follow him, the leader. Peter was given to expressing his loyalty to the Master, rather boastfully, saying that even if others deserted him, he would not. How wrong he was became obvious when he denied Jesus three times. His brashness, if one may call it that, made him unafraid of friend or foe. He even chided the Master: "And Peter took him aside and began to rebuke him (Jesus)" Matt 16: 22. One cannot but appreciate the team culture, which the Master inculcated. Peter takes Jesus 'aside' to rebuke him. Not in the presence of others. We are tempted to put Peter down as the right-brain type - emotional, impulsive, brash, given to angry outbursts and rather predictable in his responses. His head was most often half a step behind his heart. Yet, his fire-in-the-belly attitude endeared him to both Master and the rest of the team. Could that have prompted his selection as successor to Jesus? It is difficult to state with certainty. But it is clear that Jesus had confidence in him (Matt 16:18). With practical wisdom Goethe wrote: "Treat a man as he is and he will remain as he is; treat a man as he can and should be, and he will become as he can and should be?" Would these words apply also to the way Jesus groomed Peter? Look at what became of Peter in the caring hands of the Master!

Only after Jesus had died and risen, did they fully

understand the true nature of the Kingdom he was setting in motion. It was primarily a spiritual kingdom and not a political power, as most of them expected and wanted. He put in place a simple plan of action that could be achieved using basic talents, skills and faith in him. With the changed understanding came a transformation; a dramatic change. Compare the cowering apostles portrayed in the Gospels, with the bold and confident characters in the Acts of the Apostles (a latter part of the New Testament) and we see them perform works of extraordinary courage, to the admiration of the common folk, and the consternation of those in power.

It is the General who makes warriors of soldiers.

The Golden Rule

Chapter 7

Jesus and Professionals

"The Leader must be everything that he desires his subordinates to become. Men think as their leaders think and most know unerringly how their leader thinks."

~ General Sumerall

In chapters 5 and 6 we watched Jesus perform. We marveled at the many sides of his towering personality and were edified with the wonders he performed in relating to people and situations. Now, it is time to draw inferences for us, professionals. Can we learn from him? Can he be a model?

HOW DOES JESUS' MISSION CONNECT WITH PROFESSIONALS?

a) The message of **love** is universal; it is for all – professionals are not excluded. The first part of the message is to love God. Loving God is the choice each makes. Many are happy loving him. Some try to deny him. Some others are

The Golden Rule

indifferent. They think that they can exclude God from their lives. Although they want to wriggle out of God's embrace, his arms encircle all; he makes no exceptions. The choice is theirs to accept Him or not. But loving others, which is the second part, is not optional. Why? The psychiatrist Alfred Adler has the answer: "All human failures are the result of a lack of love". When we refuse to love and help others, why would they love and help us? It is stating the obvious that we need others in the network of life; even as others need us. We are de-bonded when we do not hold helping hands and when we refuse to clasp imploring hands. We need our families, our employers, our peers, our customers and many others. No one is outside the loop; and we are in the loop that others construct. The brotherhood of man, like the Fatherhood of God, is as vital as the air we breathe. The third part in the message on love is love of self. Thankfully, we need no coaxing to love ourselves.

    b) We may love others without having to serve them. But we cannot genuinely **serve** others without loving them. We cannot serve our families and our professional associates without respecting their interests. When (b) – serving others – is in place, then (a) - loving others – has gone ahead. The two

– (a) and (b) - work together. When we treat every relationship as a customer-relationship, in our interest and that of the corporation, we will build goodwill, culminating in customer-delight, and profit from such transactions.

c) Getting **wrong-doers** to repent and mend their ways may appear to be outside our professional purview. But in truth it is not. How do we explain that? Why do we have appraisals in the professional context, if not to suggest improvement; if not to correct those who err? Why should we worry over failing performances of our colleagues? Why should we take credit for positive performance of team mates, when we counsel them? Why do we try to repeatedly correct those who are in our team? It is because we fall when they fall. To stop them from falling we must use our strength and capabilities. No, we professionals cannot turn away from **wrong-doers** or poor performers.

WHAT IS THE MESSAGE FOR PROFESSIONALS DRAWN FROM JESUS' BELIEFS?

In Corporate circles, Jesus' teachings and his beliefs may seem idealistic, rather impracticable. He silences his detractors with a parable of huge dimensions; pragmatic dimensions: "He

The Golden Rule

put before them another parable: The kingdom of heaven may be compared to someone who sowed good seeds in his field; but while everybody was asleep, an enemy came and sowed weeds among the wheat, and then went away. So when the plants came up and bore grain, then the weeds appeared as well. And the slaves of the householder came and said to him, 'Master, did you not sow good seed in your field? Where, then did these weeds come from?' He answered, 'An enemy has done this.' The slaves then said to him, 'Then do you want us to go and gather them?' But he replied, 'No; for in gathering the weeds you would uproot the wheat along with them. Let both of them grow together until the harvest; and at harvest time I will tell the reapers, collect the weeds first and bind them in bundles to be burned, but gather the wheat in to my barn'" Matt 13:24-30. We cannot but admire his discerning response. Wait. There are times we shall have to suffer some evil in the larger interests of operations, but not for long. A predetermined compromise will have to be made for long term gains. Not in principles. Not in basics. No. There will be no compromise on truth, on integrity and so on; but in strategies, to meet and beat competition. He does not forget the practical side.

Chapter 7 | Jesus and Professionals

The Gospels recount many more beliefs Jesus shared with his listeners. But we have listed only six here (from chapter 5), to focus on the ones that significantly affect the world of professionals. Let us find out how they translate into a message for professionals:

a) **The Golden Rule:** Professionals, like many of us, pursue their interests at the cost of others. They must win. Losing is not an option. To win they will adopt any means. Winning makes them smug. They climb the victory stand to applause that is deafening. But deep down are they happy? One wonders. If they face themselves, as they should, they may find dark recesses in them that need light. Some parts in them are alien to the whole. That is why the Golden Rule makes sense. We cannot find joy in walking over others. We cannot live in peace with pyrrhic victories. We must value others as we value ourselves and adopt the win-win attitude. If we do not like to be walked over, how does it make sense to walk over others? When we treat others badly, we give them reason to retaliate. The Golden Rule is not just for the weak who cannot fight back, because they will be overpowered, but for the strong as well, who have the power to quell dissent. It is for all – professionals

The Golden Rule

and non-professionals.

b) **One cannot serve two masters:** One cannot serve God and Satan at the same time. One cannot compromise on ethics and believe that operations are clean. One cannot be deceitful and put on a straight face at the same time. One cannot ignore fair play and expect fairness from others. Duplicity will exact a price sooner than later. Professional choices have to be right – in the short and long term.

c) **To be wise:** Many professionals pride themselves in being clever, smart, on top of all they do. It is a nice feeling; but an empty feeling. Unless they are wise (and we all know what that means) their deeds will haunt them, because short term gains do not live long term. Expediency is fraught with risks. And down the road there is always someone smarter. **Honesty and Fidelity as expressions of wisdom:** In an Indian vernacular, a saying is: 'The one who cheats repeatedly will be caught soon'. History has shown it to be true. Disclosures of wrong doing in the professional world no more surprise us – they happen every day. We have lost our sense of **honesty** and sin. Therefore we justify our actions. Our conscience is appeased with the argument that everyone is doing it; it is okay. Distressingly, our children use the same logic. With that we perpetuate wrong doing.

And **fidelity** to the corporation is not negotiable. Grouses over pay and perks, unhappiness on how we are treated, dissatisfaction with unfair company policies and fatigue over long hours do not justify unfaithfulness or betrayal. If the burden is too heavy, shed it; move to a place where expectations are met, but do not stay dissatisfied and betray the company. It is a test of character to be honest and true.

d) **Attitude to wealth:** The temptation to make unlawful gains is irresistible; the logic compelling – many others are doing it and apparently happy. We stain our hands and cannot wash them clean. Why does this happen? The inordinate attachment we have towards profit, possessions and pleasure drive us into acts we would not normally perform. Sane men go insane under the influence of such attachments. And professionals are no exception.

e) **Attitude to enemies:** The pity is that competition is regarded as an enemy to be crushed under-foot. To achieve that end we will employ fair or foul means; more often than not the means are unwarranted. To silence the competitor within the organization, we will scheme and plot his/her downfall. Are we in peace after that? Should we not reckon with the enemy, who is plotting our downfall; who is pulling out long knives? Where will this senseless battle end? Would it not be better to adopt the abundance mentality 'of live and let live'? Would it not be better to be gracious and absolve others who wrong us? Leave them to worry on why we forgave them.

f) **Truth:** Is the choice of being truthful open to debate? Is the path of truth shrouded by doubt when millions of dollars are involved? When a coveted position is at stake? When personal loss is imminent? If it is a question of personal priority and convenience, what lessons shall we teach those who hope to learn from us - our children; our juniors? Only the truth will set us free; and our children free.

IS JESUS' KNOWLEDGE A YARDSTICK FOR PROFESSIONALS?

Can professionals be inspired by the knowledge Jesus had? They can, when they decide to gain knowledge of their functions, products, markets, competition and people. The

Chapter 7 | Jesus and Professionals

knowledge they have, when translated into strategies and implemented faithfully will bring them the desired results. Jesus showed how his knowledge amazed others. Professionals can use their great knowledge to astound themselves and the competition. Knowledge is always strength.

WHAT CAN PROFESSIONALS LEARN FROM THE WORK HABITS OF JESUS?

Management thinkers of old and of present times insist on the same basics: go to the customer and not wait for him to come to you; plan operations in detail and work that plan; and always take your people with you. The work habits that Jesus had were the same, though he operated 2000 years ago. It only shows that he was far ahead of his times. In fact he set the stage for professionals of all time – they have something to follow.

Most professionals try to work hard; plan their work and work their plan. But the question remains: What are their motives? Their interests are to be safe guarded – there is no doubt. But do the interests of others figure in their calculations? Does their own Corporation rank high on their list of priorities? Will their hard work benefit others, even as it rewards them?

The Golden Rule

Jesus answered all these questions in his faultless life when he showed that others mattered; his motives were beyond question.

WHAT CAN PROFESSIONALS LEARN FROM HIS TEAM MANAGEMENT?

Roger Dow and Susan Cook make some interesting points in their book, Turned On (Harper Business). They insist that the Team leader should keep the team focused on the big picture. He should get them pulling on the same side by connecting each to the other. And communicate with them to get them involved in goal accomplishment. They go on to make the point that a leader should be a good human being. Winston Churchill, Martin Luther King Jr., and Mother Teresa had very different styles, but each, essentially a good person, could get people to rally round a cause. The leader's integrity and strength of character secure the trust and dedication of his people. Ann Landers puts it appropriately: "Character is what you are willing to do when the spotlight has been turned off, the applause has died down and no one is around to give you credit". Character is that intangible that is tangible in the leader. The Gospels recount occasions when Jesus was acclaimed, but he shied away from recognition. He shunned the spotlight.

Chapter 7 | Jesus and Professionals

Commenting on the facets of leadership, Dow and Cook state that leaders come in different shapes and sizes. It is not the title that makes a leader, but his attributes and commitment. Leaders see themselves as resource persons - teaching, inspiring and motivating the team. Essentially, by setting the right example and by caring deeply about the team. The picture they paint of a leader has shades that mix so well that one can only behold the finished work with admiration. Now look at the shades they pick: "I think you must be a little bit strict, a little bit strong, a lit bit friendly and a little bit encouraging". A little bit of each shade to paint the picture perfect.

How does Jesus match the picture of a leader that the authors paint? With Jesus, his Mission was paramount. His chosen apostles were persuaded to understand and accept the Mission. He gave them specific instructions, so they knew what to do even in tough times. On the one hand he empowered them; on the other he held them accountable. In time, his Mission became their Guiding Principle. Many of the apostles died as martyrs for the cause. That may read like an anti-climax. Is martyrdom success? In their lexicon it was because they did not measure their success by wealth and fame, but by standards that Jesus set for them,

The Golden Rule

which was to live a life of love and die loving even those who put them to death. Strange, but lofty!

Jesus ensured that the Apostles mixed freely. He made small teams handle special assignments. He reminded them of their unique role; that they were chosen for a great purpose. He instilled confidence in them and built on their strengths, gently correcting them. He identified with them. He was with them for most of the three years of his public ministry, leading by example; teaching, clarifying, demonstrating to them. He did not ignore even matters of little importance. He delegated responsibility with authority; and molded the team into a cohesive whole. The four Gospels have several passages to show his deep caring and constant concern. He reached out to his team, consoling, encouraging, educating and helping them. He listened, empathized and readily forgave. He cared even when it hurt him most. In essentials, he fostered unity; in non-essentials, he gave them liberty; and in everything he embraced them in love. From him they learnt that 'life is love's brief tournament'.

In chapter 6 we read of the different facets of his team management. In choosing his team, his charisma came into play. It is important for recruiters to remember that. The profile of the company helps, but the charisma of the interviewer casts a spell on the candidate. Jesus chose to keep the team structure lean, simple and effective. Professionals need to guard against many levels in a structure. Too many create a distance, too few take away a healthy distance. To find the right structure is a test of professional maturity. Jesus managed his weak team through a combination of different but effective methods. Situational Management. Today's professionals are urged to follow in his footsteps, because managing a weak team is more taxing and challenging than getting results out of a gifted team.

Some of the methods Jesus adopted were:

a) Getting his team to commit to his mission.

b) Through that he gained their obedience.

c) To give them confidence in him, he continually sprang to their defence, so that they felt secure in his leadership.

d) Without a superior stance, he treated each differently to make them feel wanted.

e) He struck a fine balance between freedom and

discipline – giving them a sense of friendish without familiarity.

f) Always leading by example, he understood each of them and responded to their needs, so much so, they identified with him.

g) Besides delegating responsibilities, he planned for succession, so that there would be no void when he left.

(This is an abridged version of the message Jesus gave professionals. The unabridged version is spread across the chapters that follow.)

Chapter 8
Appraising Relationships

"Assuredly nobody will care for him who cares for nobody."

~ Thomas Jefferson.

Bangalore is about 200 miles from Chennai (earlier known as Madras), India. It is a short journey by train. Susan was planning to make that trip and was packing a few belongings and gifts for her visit to Bangalore. She was to leave town for two days. James, Alex's brother, had bought a new apartment in Bangalore and was moving in. He had invited Alex and his family to join him in the celebrations. Alex could not go. He had important customers due on Saturday, though it was the weekend. Susan and son Antony would go instead. They would leave on Friday night and return on Monday morning. Antony would have to skip a day at school, if they arrived late. The prospect pleased him.

Alex was reconciled to the idea of spending the weekend alone. Catching up on some reading and dashing off some personal mails. His plans would soon go awry. On Friday morning, Victor checked in but left in a hurry. He was not feeling well. He called Alex and made his excuses. The meeting scheduled for Friday afternoon would have to be rescheduled. Would he please explain to the other VPs? Maya would call each of the others and do some explaining.

"We'll have to fix another time." Victor was apologetic.

"No problem," Alex reassured him. And enquired: "How would Sunday suit you?"

"That should be fine by me. We'll have to check with the others."

"Susan is out of town and I am alone. Perhaps we could meet at my place. We'll be left to ourselves."

"That is superb. But check with the others."

"Maya will call you at home and get your approval after we have sounded out the others", Alex suggested.

"Okay." Victor hung up.

So Sunday it was. They were to meet at Alex's house in the morning and freewheel. The discussion could just go on and on.

Chapter 8 | Appraising Relationships

There would be no order or sequence in the discussion; just random thoughts, expressed without inhibition. Joseph would stand by to fetch them short-eats, tea and other odds and ends, to keep body fires burning.

At 11-05, the meeting started with Victor apologizing for the postponement. He hinted that the rescheduling could have given them, very providentially, more time to read the New Testament and the other reading material that he had given them. He requested Deepak to make notes.

"Out of some evil much good comes," he philosophized.

"Yes, I read through Mathew and Mark and the other sheets," Deepak announced.

"I also have read those." Andy joined in.

"I am one step ahead. I read Mathew, Mark and Luke, besides the other papers." Sammy scored.

"I have read the Gospels many times. My mother saw to it. But I have not reflected on it the way Victor has." Alex was modest.

Only Gaps had not spoken. All eyes turned to him. With

The Golden Rule

customary caution he began.

"You see, when we spoke on Wednesday I was rather abrupt. Rather unprofessional. Victor's note struck a chord in me. I argued with myself. After all we were not into a religious discourse; we were looking at only professional stuff. Could we find something in Jesus? Jesus could be wise. What was wrong in looking at his wisdom, if he had some to offer? I convinced myself that I was wrong. I owe you an apology for my terse reactions. Now, to give you proof of my goodwill let me tell you, like Victor, I read the four Gospels and the extra sheets he gave us."

Victor put his hands together and started a slow clap. The others joined in. The applause was spontaneous. Gaps colored. Putting up his hands he said: "Thank you. You are kind."

"Now that we have started well, why not Gaps lead the discussion?" Victor suggested.

Gaps protested and so did other VPs. Victor should lead. And that stayed.

"Okay, the team decision will be honored." Victor gave in.

"So how shall we put points together?" he asked cleverly,

ensuring that the lead went back to his team.

"Perhaps by attempting a 360° appraisal of Jesus," Deepak proposed.

"That is brilliant, absolutely brilliant; no better way to do it." Victor was bullish on the idea.

"That's a great idea," Andy echoed.

"So why don't you start, Deepak?" Victor urged.

"A word of caution: since we do not know how the 360° appraisal is administered in India, we have to be rather careful in stating our opinions. In applying the system, we are not even novices. So let us go about it cautiously. It may seem okay because we are looking at a person in history. Even so, we have to be fair in our assessment." Deepak was solemn.

"Said like a true HR man," Alex complimented.

"The 90° appraisal is not possible because Jesus reported to no one. For feedback from peers, teammates and customers, we have plenty of evidence in the Gospels." Deepak looked for support. And heads nodded.

Victor stepped in: "Unless, we place Pilate, the Roman

Governor, in the role of a superior."

Alex spoke up: "Even if we do, Pilate found no fault in Jesus. He was visibly impressed with his regal behavior, and tried hard to set him free. Because Pilate was a coward he succumbed to public pressure."

Gaps shared an insight: "You are right, Alex. What struck me in the four Gospels is that Pontus Pilate the Roman Governor, a very senior professional in the Roman hierarchy, is not the one who inspires us (professionals), but the one he condemned to crucifixion and death. Pilate the professional is dwarfed in the presence of the super-professional, Jesus. The irony is confounding."

"That is a profound observation, Gaps," Victor admiringly stated.

"So, the first quadrant gets 'favorable remarks. Is that okay by all?" Deepak was looking for quick general agreement. There were approving glances.

But Andy interjected: "Are we not rushing it?"

To which Victor replied: "You are right. But these are only

our first thoughts on the subject."

Deepak continued: "To my mind we should begin with his teammates. What did they have to say? That is, if we categorize the apostles as subordinates".

"To help us along I have flagged pages and underlined some passages," Sammy offered support.

"We should learn to do our homework like Sammy," Victor applauded.

"Not only Sammy, I also have used a highlighter for important passages." Gaps took a spot of glory, as approving smiles greeted him.

"What struck me about Jesus was his strong conviction," Andy initiated.

"Reminds me of the words of Robert Townsend of Avis: 'Things get done in our society because of a man or woman with conviction,'" Victor supported Andy's statement; and continued: "Unlike us who buckle under threats or who yield to pressure, Jesus stood firm. Threats to his person, ridicule from important people, fear that his disciples would leave him - none of these made Jesus change his beliefs and teaching. His resolve was firm. And his actions reinforced his words. He was consistent. That is a lesson for us."

"Perhaps his maturity stood out," Andy suggested.

"What would you call maturity?" Sammy interrogated.

"On behalf of Andy I'll try and answer that. I cannot offer a comprehensive definition. To my mind maturity is a happy mix of conviction and empathy. The mature person decides and acts with conviction that blends with consideration for other people". Deepak came to Andy's rescue.

"By that standard are we mature?" Alex asked, fishing for some feedback from Victor on his appraisal.

"We shall certainly discuss that when we come to our appraisals. For now, let us check how Jesus measures on the maturity scale." Victor tactfully answered him. "Was he mature? Did he combine conviction with empathy?" Victor probed.

"Loads of it," Sammy replied confidently. "The word 'compassion' is repeated so often in the Gospels. A compassionate person empathizes. Of that we have no doubt," Sammy continued, with shop-floor experience.

"The Gospels use the word compassion often. But I like to believe that the writers really meant empathy. When one has compassion, pity for the plight of the suffering person follows and there is a desire to pour out succor to the one suffering; not quite checking if he wants to receive it the way it is given. One tends to lose sight of the receiver's self-respect, when pity motivates the act. In empathy, there is feeling of a higher order. One tends to identify oneself with the suffering person, and visualize his feelings, his experience. One becomes more sensitive to the way the other person feels. Put simply, one gets into his shoes. Then one does not force down help. Instead one checks how the person in need would want it. That is precisely how Jesus acted when anyone came to him for help. He asked the suffering person what he wanted. Only then did he respond. And he responded promptly. He responded the way the suffering person sought succor. He empathized. In contrast, what do we do? We extend help grudgingly, take credit for it, and show no concern for the person we tried to help. Did he benefit from the help we gave? It does not concern us." They all heard Deepak with great admiration.

"Deepak, you picture us as heartless people. But that is a

The Golden Rule

fact. We really do not care enough." Andy said, thoughtfully.

"Even those who teased him with awkward questions were not answered in anger, though he fittingly replied them," Gaps joined in.

"Look at the way he managed his apostles; his team," Sammy added.

"Who were these men? Ordinary fisher folk whom he transformed," he continued.

"He used Situational Management. Not a fixed style; always adapting to the situation and the person; understanding the needs of the apostle and serving that need." Victor recalled what Alex had told him a few days ago on the Situational Management style that he was trying to adopt.

"Deepak's check-list will have all these points, no doubt," Victor announced.

"Let us not drift. We'll keep to what we wanted to examine. What his subordinates, the apostles had to say of him," Deepak corrected course.

"Deepak, we want to stay on course. But since we are

freewheeling let our thoughts take us along for a while." Victor pleaded.

"Right then, what is it going to be?" Deepak questioned.

"Look at us; you, Alex and me; in fact all of us. Our high priced shoes, expensive branded suits, classy ties, cell phones, computers, credit cards, business class air travel, five-star hotel stay, holiday resorts and bulging wallets. Not forgetting our fancy designations and flashy cars; all our props. What would we be without these props? How effective would we be? How would others see us? How would we see ourselves? Chances are that we are seen as pretenders." Victor stressed his words, in a challenging mood.

There was a pregnant pause as each let his thoughts roam. What would it really look like, bereft of executive-trappings? Look like hollow men in branded clothes; weird.

"Almost naked," Alex said despondently.

"Naked! What a thought?" Gaps shuddered.

"And look at Jesus. He wore the simplest of clothes. No proper place to lodge; wandering gypsy-like from village to village, town to town; and yet he stayed focused; fully focused and gained more respect than we do." Victor spoke with feeling.

"But that was a very different period." Andy halted Victor.

"You are right. But think of it. Surely there were others more ceremoniously dressed, with titles to their names and an animal to move around; a mule or a horse. Many had a better living standard and some cash to spend. Jesus had none of these and gained more respect than those who had much. What was his secret?" Victor would not give up.

"That is a fine way of looking at it," Sammy agreed.

"What was his secret?" Victor repeated.

"His charisma, his character and his personality, accounted for it," Sammy suggested, and continued: "His character being sober, dignified and dependable, he built trust. His charisma was such that when he said: 'Follow me', they followed him. Not just the fisherman, but also the tax collector. His personality was seen in consistently mature behavior in different situations."

"He radiated confidence, which came from deep inside. No bravado. He spoke with authority. So, the people said. He was accessible to the poor and the rich. Perhaps those qualities gave him strong charismatic appeal." Gaps expanded.

"Peter Drucker had much to say on character. A person without character destroys. He destroys people, destroys spirit and destroys performance." Drucker was a favorite with Deepak.

"That is why the character of Jesus drew people to him. His character made him stand out among others who were mostly pretenders and power brokers." Andy reasoned.

"That is true." Victor affirmed.

"So he stood tall even without props. We need all our props because we lack his sterling qualities. Would that be safe to assume?" Sammy questioned.

"I agree. After reading the Gospels we seem more like pygmies in the presence of a giant," Andy admitted modestly.

"Can we now get back to his apostles? What they had to say?" Deepak sounded impatient.

"Why, were we not discussing Jesus?" Victor teased.

"Yes we were; but off our agenda." Deepak reasoned.

"We shall now get to the apostles and what they thought

The Golden Rule

of Jesus." Victor affirmed.

"Not so fast," Sammy interjected. "I want a word in. Victor, you used the word 'focused'. That Jesus was focused."

"Yes. I did." Victor concurred.

"What was he focused on?" Sammy demanded.

"He was focused on his mission and therefore his daily work had a purpose and a meaning. Consider his mission. You recall that we read about it in the material we received. It had three parts. The three parts sprang from the main mission. The first part was the ushering in of a new order. An order founded on love; love of God and his fellowmen. From this emerged the other two: service to fellowmen and reconciliation with wrong-doers. The second and third are sequels to the first. If one had love, the rest followed. Jesus was focused all the time on his Mission. He knew why he was here and let no distractions come in the way. Even when people were so impressed with him and wanted to crown him as their King, he declined the high office and remained focused on his mission. What about us? We are seldom focused. The slightest distraction takes us away from our goal, our schedule and our routine. We are a dissipated lot."

Chapter 8 | Appraising Relationships

"After reading the Gospels and admiring the qualities of Jesus, our self-worth is taking a beating. Don't you think?" queried Sammy.

"Yes. I think so too. But I am encouraged by the fact that such introspection will help us change; grow. Unless we know our weaknesses, we cannot improve." Victor agreed.

"Is love of fellowmen supposed to cover even the opposition?" Gaps shot off at a tangent.

"Yes. When he said 'love your enemies' he meant that; and showed how." Victor explained.

"How would you use that in the Market place, Alex?" Gaps pursued.

"Alex, may I answer that for you?" Victor requested. Alex looked pleased.

"That is a tricky question, Gaps. But let us see how it should work; not how it works. My competitor is doing his job, as I am doing mine. For me to hate him and pull him down because he is in the opposite camp is pointless. I might not agree with him, but I don't have to malign him. 'You have to compete and co-operate at the same time.' Aren't those the words of Raymond Noorda, the former CEO of Novell? For example, we could end up on the same side of the table when our united efforts in Industry could explain common problems to the Government or other bodies; our joint efforts could clear wrong ideas on product categories. Because of our competitors we push ourselves to perform better. In other words, we need our competitors for strength. In a way, competition does us a good turn. So, instead of despising them, we should try to understand them. Look at Jesus. The Pharisees and Sadducees and other groups looked for ways to snare him and undermine him. How did he respond? He exposed hypocrisy (as we should) but extended a hand in friendship. He faulted the deceit, not the deceiver. He accused the manipulation, not the manipulator. He begged the sinner not to sin again; but forgave the sinner readily. I see no contradiction in his mission and the opposition. It is a question of understanding the Mission and applying it sensibly even to competition."

"Great defense, Victor," commended Alex. Victor smiled in acknowledgement.

"If what you say is the new way we should look at competition, I am for it. Though I am in finance and not in the market place, I see needless hostility. We could do without some of it," Andy inferred.

"That is a spurring thought. Let our corporation give a lead in pulling down barriers that artificially separate us in Industry. The market is big enough for all of us not only to survive, but to prosper." The leader in Victor surfaced.

"Would the all-embracing love of Jesus explain his detachment to material possessions? He owned little or nothing. He craved for nothing." Andy stated matter-of-factly.

"Here again we should interpret the passages in the right context. He did not want money or material possessions. He loved his mother. In fact, the first miracle he performed was at her behest. Yet he planned to leave her no material legacy. His attitude to money was rather simple. Money is necessary. It has a role to play. But do not get attached to money, he cautioned. Don't become a slave to money, he admonished. Don't let it become an obsession, he warned. He praised the thrifty. He commended the resourceful and enterprising. He chided wasteful behavior. What a contrast to the way we see things! For us stock prices reflect the health of the company. We even twist

The Golden Rule

accounting to manipulate stock prices. Sales and profits tell us how well we are doing. Reserves indicate how secure our future could be. We are mystified by numbers, not by substance. We are captivated with winning at all costs." Gaps connected well.

"How should we apply that in the corporate world?" Andy wanted to know.

"Make profits. Yes. We owe it to our company to make justifiable profits. But profiteering; no; cutting corners to make profit; no; illegal ways of making profit; no. With the profits we make we have some social concerns to address. Don't we expect rich nations to help poor nations? In the same way, corporations doing well, have a responsibility to return something to society, not just by way of taxes. In a way helping society is enlightened self-interest. A more developed society becomes a more responsive market for new products. An improved life-style is fertile ground for planting innovative ideas. The enlightened self-interest apart, we owe it to those around us that we share something with them. The examples of Bill Gates and Warren Buffet should inspire us. They make enormous profits, but readily distribute substantial sums in charity. Simply put, fascination with an improving bottom line is good as long as we are not enslaved

Chapter 8 | Appraising Relationships

by it. It is difficult to follow. But try, we shall". Victor spoke those words with a rare vehemence. He had always held in private and in public that a corporate citizen had more than ordinary obligations to society.

"Since Jesus was detached from wealth and possessions, he could look at people and circumstances objectively." Gaps proposed.

"True. Take his golden rule. Do to others as you would have them do to you. That was possible because he was objective and fair, not affected by labels and always sworn to love." Victor had it all tied up.

"Is that possible in our corporate situations?" Gaps raised a doubt.

"It is very, very difficult; sometimes almost impossible. And yet it makes sense. When I say that, I am aware that I cannot equate transactions that I may have with my chauffeur, to transactions I may have with my suppliers or buyers. There will be a difference. The tragedy today is the total lack of respect for those without proper labels. I quickly adjust to the rank or status of the person in front of me. I respect and respond to a label. That is where my duplicity is exposed. What I need to do is to realize that behind each label, big or small, is a person. And that person begs to be treated with some dignity. He wants a voice, which we silence. It is our harsh response that leads to disparities. Our double standards are exposed. Jesus pleaded that we do away with our double standards." Victor was persuasive.

"Perhaps that is why Jesus did not abuse the power he had." Andy deduced.

"To begin with, we should try to understand what we mean by power and authority. Some experts define power as the ability to influence beliefs and actions of others; and authority, as the right to make decisions affecting others. Take Jesus. He had enormous power. He worked wondrous deeds and communicated effectively. His knowledge was praised. His power was seen time and again. But did he abuse that power? People were literally eating out of his hands, and yet it was always: 'if you believe' and 'your faith has made you whole'. No pressure, not even subtle pressure to convert. With his powers he could have performed miracles when he was arrested and taken before the high priests and Pilate. To save himself he could have performed the magic they were waiting for and stunned his audience. No; he would not use cheap gimmicks. He believed in placing facts before people, expecting them to decide, without a trace of compulsion. No, he did not use his enormous powers to influence people to his thinking. Real power is when you have it and restrain yourself in using it; be prudent and empathetic in exercising it. And of his authority, we see disciplined use. He asked his disciples to follow a particular code. When they failed, he was gentle and forgiving. With others it was always, 'what would you want me do for you?' The option rested with the other person. Jesus responded when they chose an option or made a request. His authority was never oppressive. You are right Andy Jesus did not abuse his power. We have only to look at the way we transact, to admire Jesus. We exercise the little power we have with a sense of bravado. We want people to fear us, because we have some power. And our display of authority is almost vulgar. But we are quick to bow before someone in higher authority. Our use of power and authority is a sham." Deepak was emphatic.

Gaps was ready with the next question: "As I read the four Gospels a question that puzzled me was, why did Jesus not marry and raise a family like Rabbis of his time or some of his apostles?"

Victor offered to answer him. "That is a difficult question.

The Golden Rule

But I'll try to answer it. Jesus should have had good reasons for staying single. The Gospels do not provide us with any reasons for his choice, but we could make some assumptions which conform with his personality and mission. One, Jesus knew that his life was short. So, leaving behind a young wife and perhaps tiny children did not seem a good option to one who was full of empathy. Two, his work took him from place to place. He could not settle in one town. He could not sink roots. His family, if he had one, would suffer from neglect. Even his mother, whom he loved dearly, could spend time with him rarely, because he was constantly moving from town to town. Three, his mission was his prime focus. If he took on family responsibilities his mission-efforts would receive less time and attention. He could not let that happen. Four, he was not in a job or profession which gave him earnings. He had given up his work as a carpenter to make time for his mission. With no income his family would be put to unending financial difficulty. As a wandering rabbi, he depended on the generosity of his followers and listeners to keep body and soul together. Five, the Gospels portray him as the Son of God. Therefore, an earthly family would not fit his Divine program, so to speak. I am not sure, but I believe that our assumptions could be the reasons why Jesus chose to remain single. It appears that he did not want to start a relationship that he could not nurture. He was careful not to take on anything that he could not complete."

Gaps: "Thank you, Victor. Your assumptions are logical."

Alex's hand phone buzzed. Susan was calling. The day went well at his brother's place - with grand celebrations. They all missed him and wished he was there. They were leaving by the night train, and would be in on Monday morning. And Antony wanted to say hello to daddy. The call over, Alex checked his watch. It was ten past one. Joseph fetched the short eats and drinks. The sight of food and drink was refreshing. Breaking off from the serious discussion, they teased Victor on his weight gain and suggested he join a Gym; at least jog. He promised to start jogging, but disliked the idea of the Gym.

Gaps asked Victor if he planned to continue the discussion in the afternoon. He was willing to stay on; but what about the others? Since none of the others had engagements in the afternoon they all decided to continue with the discussions. At least until 3.30 or 4 pm. When the trolley was cleared, Deepak cleared his throat and declared officially: "We shall now get down to what the apostles had to say". The group went into a fit of laughter.

"Why do we have to rush?" Victor enquired of Deepak.

"I was beginning to wonder whether we would get back at all." Deepak was not amused.

"Deepak is right. Now we stick to the 360° appraisal for Jesus. Let us hear what the apostles had to say." Victor was apologetic.

"Thomas said that they (the apostles) should go and die with Jesus. Or take Peter; he asked Jesus where else they could go, but to him. Or again, Peter declared that they had left everything and followed him. Or Mathew; he gave up his job as a tax collector to follow Jesus. Each showed a readiness to accept his leadership; to obey him and to accept correction. He offered them no money, no fame, only 'take up your cross and follow me'. And they followed". Gaps had read the New Testament in full and could marshal facts.

"What we are trying to say is that his Team Management skills were of a high order and therefore feedback from the team was edifying," Sammy concluded.

Chapter 8 | Appraising Relationships

"Are we then agreed that in the third quadrant we put down, 'very good'," Deepak tossed the idea in the open.

"For now, that should be all right. Since the 360° appraisal focuses on relationships, and we are examining the possibility of setting up Jesus as a Model for our relationships, we shall have to review our assessments and appraisal as we learn more of him." Victor was cautious.

"What had his peers to say?" Sammy asked.

"John the Baptist, Nicodemus, Joseph of Arimathea, the Centurion and Zacchaeus are seen as important peers; since they held important positions in society, their statements should throw some light. Each one treated Jesus with great respect. And admiration." Gaps again had his facts right.

"Don't we see any discord; for example, from the High priests?" Andy challenged.

"The High priests were people in high positions, no doubt. But they had vested interests. Jesus was attracting crowds, and creating a sensation. The High priests felt threatened. Naturally, they would not speak kindly of the man they feared. One cannot lay store by what they had to say. The close attention they paid to the feedback they got on him, if at all, can be seen as a grudging tribute paid to Jesus," Gaps reasoned.

"The enlightened and fair minded peers had only good things to say of Jesus. Is that what you wish to convey, Gaps?" Deepak asked pointedly.

"Yes," Gaps was decisive.

"In which case, what comment shall we put down in quadrant two, against peers?" Deepak asked, ready to take down points.

"Let it be 'good'," Victor suggested.

"Why not 'very good?'" Deepak demanded.

"As I said earlier, we shall review this later. For now let us retain 'good', unless someone has strong reason to give it a different remark." Victor was defensive.

Alex looked at the others. They shrugged their shoulders and decided to go along. So it stayed as 'good' with the appropriate elaboration Deepak would give it.

"The fourth relationship is perhaps the most important. The customers, how did they see him?" This question should have come from Alex, the marketing man instead it came from Andy, the finance man.

"Those who were influenced by the opposite camp chose to make derogatory statements, but the others had only praise. They praised his gentle ways; marveled at his great deeds; were amazed at his new teaching. And his communication skill cast a spell on them." Victor glowed.

"Those he came to serve are seen as his customers. And feedback from them is positive; very positive. Only those who tried to trap him in debate had caustic remarks to pass, more, because they could not match him and failed to expose him. So what hesitation do we have in putting down remarks in the fourth quadrant?" Sammy was impatient.

"No hesitation. What do you say Alex?" Victor queried.

"What is fine by you is fine by me." Alex was feebly courteous.

Victor looked at him and looked away. Something was wrong, he thought.

"Shall we put down 'very good' in that space?" Deepak

The Golden Rule

asked.

"Yes, 'very good' it shall be". Victor bellowed.

Deepak looked at his pad and said: "Let us quickly look at the remarks we have given Jesus in each quadrant of the 360° appraisal format. Under 'superiors' in the first quadrant we have 'positive'. Under 'peers' in the second also we have 'positive'. Under 'subordinates' in the third we have 'very positive'. And in the fourth also, under 'customers' we have 'very positive'. This is not final; only our initial reactions. I shall work on this and fill in the blanks and expand points where necessary. But if the overall assessment meets with your approval, I shall take it as approved." Deepak was trying to get his summary cleared.

Heads shook in vigorous agreement.

"May we call it a day?" Andy enquired. He had to drive a long way to his place.

"Yes. But this is not the end. We have more work to do. But for now it is over. Before you leave please collect copies of more reading material I have for you. They are titled: The People Person and Perceptions of the Model. Read them diligently. There is more information in them that we could use in the 360 degree

Chapter 8 | Appraising Relationships

appraisal – views of different people. Remember that we have to be prepared for the Marketing Conference which will be organized by Alex in the next few days. We have much to learn from Jesus and apply those lessons to our situation. Now let us get back to our families and enjoy what is left of our Sunday." Victor concluded.

The Golden Rule

Chapter 9
The People Person

"The service we render to others is really the rent we pay for our room on this earth."

~ W. Grenfell

People need to be reassured that a 'comfort-zone' operates, if they are to draw near. They must feel wanted; free to interact, with no fear of a rebuff. That is why Jesus invited people to him with soothing and reassuring words: "Come to me, all you that are weary and are carrying heavy burdens and I will give you rest" Matt 11:28. John chooses different words to convey the same warmth: "And anyone who comes to me I will never drive away" John 6:37. And people came: The poor and the needy, the sick and the handicapped, the hungry and the weak, the depressed and the dejected, saints and sinners. Mixing freely with such people he gave of his abundant generosity. He had come to serve his fellowmen. That, he would do without reserve.

The Golden Rule

What stood out in these interactions was his empathy. His heart went out to those in trouble, finding ways to comfort them (Matt 9:36).

a) Dignified in giving: Although he was compassionate beyond measure, he was careful not to force himself on them. Like a true gentleman, he checked what they wanted of him: "Then Jesus said to him, 'What do you want me to do for you?'" Mark 10: 51. When they had made their requests, he granted them what they asked for. We wonder why Jesus had to ask (for example, ask the blind man what he wanted), when he could see what the need was. Perhaps, Jesus wanted the crowd around him to know that someone had a need to which he was prepared to respond. Perhaps, by articulating his need the recipient felt he was unloading a burden. The important inference is that Jesus did not want to impose himself on anyone.

b) Humble and composed: His dignity in responding to the needs of his neighbors was born of his disarming humility. So real was his humility, that people saw it and recognized it. Even in moments of triumph he stayed composed (Mark 11:7-10) and not exultant. As he entered Jerusalem the crowds threw their clothes, cloaks and leafy branches on the road so that he could ride over them, while they shouted Hosanna. There was no vainglory; only quiet acceptance of the triumphant moment. He knew the fickleness of the crowd. In a few days those very people would scream for his crucifixion and death.

c) Forgiving wrong-doers: His ego was balanced and therefore he could view the failings of others with compassion, not accusation. The example he set onlookers from the cross, has no parallel in history. Physically abused and tortured by soldiers, reviled by crowds standing around him, deserted by friends, in pain and agony, from the crucible of pain he cries out: "Father, forgive them; for they do not know what they are doing" Luke 23:34.

Some writers compare the death of Socrates to Jesus' death. Both lost their lives at the hands of their detractors. Socrates faced his end with a potion of Hemlock. Jesus suffered excruciating pain and a shameful death on the cross. Is a quiet death equal to a brutal and violent death? The comparison is odious, all the more because of the example Jesus set from the cross. He had preached forgiveness. Now, by example he was living his teaching. His persecutors were being forgiven their malice and hard-heartedness. He gave forgiveness a new dimension when he explained to Peter that one does not keep score, instead one forgives as many times as is necessary (Matt 18:21-22).

In a parable, Jesus lays bare the consequences of not forgiving and not having mercy on others: "For this reason the Kingdom of heaven may be compared to a king who wished to settle accounts with his slaves. When he began the reckoning, one who owed him ten thousand talents was brought to him; and as he could not pay, his Lord ordered him to be sold, together with his wife and children and all his possessions, and payment to be made. So the slave fell on his knees before him, saying, 'Have patience with me, and I will pay you everything'. And out of pity for him, the Lord of that slave released him and forgave him the debt. But the same slave, as he went out came upon one of his fellow slaves who owed him a hundred denarii; and seizing him by the throat, he said, 'Pay what you owe'. Then his fellow slave fell down and pleaded with him, 'Have patience with me, and I will pay you'. But he refused; then he went and threw him into prison until he would pay the debt. When his fellow slaves saw what happened, they were greatly distressed, and they went and reported to their Lord all that had taken place. Then the Lord summoned him and said to him, 'You Wicked slave! I forgave you all that debt because you pleaded with me. Should you not have had mercy on your fellow slave, as I had mercy on you?' And in anger his Lord handed him over to be tortured until he could pay his entire debt" Matt 18:23-34.

Not forgiving those who offend us is not an option. Jesus makes that clear when he teaches his apostles to pray – The Lord's Prayer. We can expect forgiveness from God only when we forgive others. Saint Paul gives a new twist to forgiveness. He says that when you really want revenge – forgive. Why? Because when you forgive, you truly 'heap burning coals on their heads' Romans 12: 20. They have to carry the additional burden of not really knowing why they were forgiven. The metaphor of burning coals is drawn from a Roman practice – someone who is forgiven carried on his head a pan of burning coals. A forgiven soul is in perpetual debt to the one who forgives him.

d) Self-effacing: His words and deeds had such an enormous impact on people that even when he instructed them to keep his profile low, word of mouth propaganda could not be stopped. His fame spread far and wide, bringing to him wave upon wave of people. Some were so greatly influenced by him that they wanted him to be their King. But he would have none of it, because he had not come to be their King in a political sense. He had come to show them a new way of life. John silences his critics who claim that he was self-seeking and bent on popularity: "When Jesus realized that they were about to come and take him by force to make him King, he withdrew again to the mountain by himself" John 6:15.

e) Fearless: To these qualities he added fearlessness and openness. He feared no one. His idea of weathering the storm was to produce a stronger gale. Watch how he does it. "At that very hour some Pharisees came and said to him, 'Get away from here, for Herod wants to kill you.' He said to them, 'Go, and tell that fox from me---'" Luke 13: 31-32. Tale carriers would ensure that the comment reached the ears of Herod, the king; yet Jesus did not fear him. Even against the Scribes who were a powerful sect, whose favors one tried to win, he was plain and decisive in his rebuttal (Luke 20:45-46). Jesus had no need for such double-dealing power brokers. So strong was his courage of conviction, that even his adversaries, grudgingly praised it: "And you show deference to no one, but teach the way of God in accordance with the truth" Luke 20: 21. In support of his openness and honesty, he said: "I have spoken openly to the world; I have always taught in the synagogues and in the temple, where all the Jews come together. I have said nothing in secret" John 18: 20.

f) Not wanting sympathy: Because he drew strength from within, he needed little or no emotional support from without. Even in his darkest hour when everyone had forsaken him, Jesus did not look for pity or sympathy. Addressing weeping women who lined the path to Calvary he deflected attention they gave him, to get them to understand what lay in store for them: "Daughters of Jerusalem, do not weep for me, but weep for yourselves and for your children" Luke 23: 28. He did not want their tears.

g) Expecting faith: What he hoped to receive was their trust. That they have faith in him, believe his words, and acknowledge his works. Many times during his public ministry he asked those who came to him if they had faith in him, because to him that was vital. On one occasion here is how he checked: "Do you believe that I am able to do this? They said to him, 'Yes lord'" Matt 9: 28.

h) Seizing the initiative: As a people-person he believed that he should seize the initiative and not wait for the other person to step forward. In the meeting with Zacchaeus, he demonstrated how he took such initiatives (Luke 19:5). Zacchaeus, short in stature, had climbed a tree to get a glimpse of Jesus as he passed by. Now, he was an important man - the chief tax collector. But he was also an unscrupulous defrauder. He retained for himself money from the tax collection. Acting as a change agent, Jesus takes the initiative to talk to him. He did not avoid him because he was corrupt, or wait for him to start the conversation. We also recall the selection of his apostles when Jesus took the initiative, each time, to choose them.

i) Using the power of praise: How does Jesus fare in interpersonal skills? Jesus knew the power of praise and used it effectively. He readily gave praise, and extolled virtue, when he saw it. To the Centurion who showed enormous faith, he gave warm praise: "When he entered Capernaum, a centurion came to him, appealing to him and saying, 'Lord, my servant is lying at home paralyzed, in terrible distress.' And he said to him, 'I will come and cure him.' The centurion answered, 'Lord, I am not worthy to have you come under my roof; but only speak the word and my servant will be healed. For I also am a man under authority, with soldiers under me; and I say to one, `go', and he goes, and to another, `come', and he comes, and to my slave, `Do this', and the slave does it'. When Jesus heard him, he was amazed and said to those who followed him, 'Truly I tell you, in no one in Israel have I found such faith'" Matt 8: 5-10. John the Baptist, Jesus' cousin, and a prophet in his own right, showed great courage in challenging the evil ways of King Herod. Openly opposing the king, at that time, had serious consequences - imprisonment and death. But John the Baptist was fearless; and Jesus compliments him (Matt 11:11). And he extols the faith of the Canaanite woman who showed exemplary confidence when she pleaded her daughter's case with him (Matt 15:28). Even little acts of little people were recognized and praised. The poor widow could put into the temple treasury only two copper coins, which is less than a penny. Jesus praises her (Mark 12:43-44). And people with virtue, he readily held up as examples. Nathaniel, the would-be Apostle is commended because he is without deceit (John 1:47). But praise was held back when he read the minds of people and found in them evil thoughts (Matt 9:4). So, with Jesus there were no favorites. Good deeds were praised and the brazen deeds of seemingly important people were bared, for them to realize their misdeeds, repent and make amends.

He warned against over-confidence and complacency. Do not take your place for granted, he cautioned: "But many who are first will be last, and the last will be first" Mark 10: 31. Do-gooders among the Pharisees believed that their law-abiding, righteous behavior gave them the right to God's friendship. Jesus lost no time in warning them that their over-confidence would be their nemesis. God's love was a gift, he asserted.

Combining the power of praise with the potency of rewards, he made a winning formula, which was motivation at its best: "Truly I tell you none of these will lose their reward" Matt 10: 42. He promised such rewards even to his apostles. They needed such motivation because they left everything behind to follow him.

j) Resolving conflicts: Where there are people, there are conflicts. And conflicts lead to hate and hostility. What had Jesus to say? Never let differences snowball. Resolve them at once: "So when you are offering your gift at the altar, if you remember that your brother or sister has something against you, leave your gift there before the altar and go; first be reconciled to your brother or sister, and then come and offer your gift" Matt 5: 23-24. Mark his words: 'If your brother or sister has something against you' and not, 'if you have something against your brother or sister'; which meant that even if you did not have hostile feelings against the other, but s/he had some against you, go and be reconciled. Be pro-active in resolving conflicts and forgiving. And, we cannot help admiring his common sense approach to resolving a conflict face-to-face: "If another member of the church sins against you, go and point out the fault when the two of you are alone. If the member listens to you, you have regained that one. But if you are not listened to, take one or two others along with you, so that every word may be confirmed by the evidence of two or three witnesses" Matt 8: 15.

What we have seen here are the multi-faceted skills of Jesus in transacting with people, as the People-Person. He was always eager to help the poor and needy. To the hungry and weak he gave speedy relief. The depressed and dejected returned with hope and confidence. The saints were confirmed in their holiness and sinners were reconciled. He did not drive away anyone who went to him; instead he gave them rest and lightened their burden. Whatever their distress, Jesus asked them to shun worry

The Golden Rule

(Matt 6:34), because he was there to address their concerns, if only they had faith in him. He could do this for others because he himself had walked through fire. Do we not use the expression: 'he has been through the mill'? It is a tribute that we pay such a person. What we really mean is that through the trials he faced and the sufferings he endured, he has been strengthened and ennobled; and therefore a better human being. He can now understand, empathize and reach out. He can now be trusted; for trust is the ultimate tribute you can pay him. They could trust Jesus. And he would honor that trust.

Chapter 10
Perceptions of the Model

"Know then this truth, enough for man to know, virtue alone is happiness below."

~ A. Pope

Jesus was no ordinary man, though he walked among ordinary people. He walked tall. That explains why he evoked different and strong reactions among people who did not walk tall. Many openly admired him, a few felt threatened, and some did not conceal their hostility. People's reactions plunged from heady exhilaration to murderous rejection. His last days on earth included one scene of triumph when he made a grand entry into Jerusalem, as people roared their approval. But even in that tumultuous welcome Jesus sat, painfully aware that their praise was hollow and passing. Despite such opposed responses, he held out his hand in friendship. 'Have no fear, Peace be with you, Have faith' - only such words would he speak. No condescension; only compassion.

The Golden Rule

The Gospels paint a picture of Jesus in different colors – perceptions of different people.

1) Let us look at the brush strokes of **people in high places:** Pilate, the Roman Governor in Palestine, The Roman Centurion and Jarius, a leader from the Synagogue. "Then Pilate said to the chief priests and the crowds, 'I find no basis for an accusation against this man.'" Luke 23: 4. The Roman Centurion who led the soldiers in their Governor-given-assignment to crucify Jesus could not hold back his praise: "When the centurion saw what had taken place (at the crucifixion), he praised God and said 'certainly this man was innocent'" Luke 23: 47. Stiff-necked leaders of the Synagogue did not bend low before Jesus. Jairus was an exception: "Then one of the leaders of the synagogue named Jairus came and, when he saw him (Jesus), fell at his feet and begged him repeatedly" Mark 5:22.

2) Besides people in high places, Nicodemus and Joseph of Arimathea, disciples of Jesus in secret, were also **important persons and contemporaries.** After Jesus died, these men sought permission from Pilate to claim the body of Jesus for burial. They bought a hundred pounds of Myrrh and aloes to treat the bruised and battered body of their master before

burial. A few pounds would have been enough. But they would follow the dictates of their hearts. It would be a hundred pounds. The cost did not count; for here was no ordinary man who was dead. John the Baptist, a prophet who was respected by many, was in a way, a contemporary. What colors did The Baptist add to the picture? "He proclaimed, 'The one who is more powerful than I is coming after me; I am not worthy to stoop down and untie the thongs of his sandals'" Mark 1:7

3) What were the perceptions of his **disciples** (not apostles)? Two of them traveling to Emmaus had Jesus (incognito) walk with them. In ecstasy they exclaimed that their hearts were alight when he was speaking with them (Luke 24:32). We have already seen how his apostles regarded him.

4) And what did his **customers** (crowds, who packed fields and river banks and seashores to listen to him, and watch him perform wondrous deeds), have to say? What mix of colors did they use? "Jesus departed with his disciples to the sea, and a great multitude from Galilee followed him; hearing all that he was doing, they came to him in great numbers from Judea, Jerusalem, Idumea, beyond the Jordan, and the region around Tyre and Sidon" Mark 3:7-8. In chapters 4 and 5 of his Gospel, Luke uses

words that border the superlative to convey what they think of him: "All spoke well of him and were amazed at the gracious words that came from his mouth" Luke 4:22. And: "Amazement seized all of them, and they glorified God and were filled with awe, saying, 'We have seen great things today'" Luke 5:26. So strong was public opinion in his favor that those who connived to put him to death were fearful of the crowd backlash and waited for a chance to take him when he was alone: "So, he (Judas) consented and began to look for an opportunity to betray him to them (Pharisees and High Priests) when no crowd was present" Luke 22:6.

Often, crowds are silk on one side and sand paper on the other. Manipulated by vested interests, they turned unfriendly now and again (John 7:12). One can connect the swing in their emotions with the way Jesus polarized opinions by boldly contrasting his teachings with the words and actions of his opponents. To assail him with questions and verbal traps, spies were planted among onlookers. Jesus knew he was not safe anywhere, but could not avoid the crowds because they sought him everywhere. The antipathy of the crowds wore off quickly and they were back listening, applauding, being fed and healed, and following him in large numbers. Many times they tried to make him king, but he would not accept glory on their terms. In truth, he sought no glory at all. Despite his attempts to stifle publicity that his actions merited, the power-brokers felt threatened, and huddled in scheming and plotting (Mark 11:11). Their apparent triumph at the crucifixion looked jaded as the criminal, hanging from a cross next to Jesus, proclaimed that Jesus was guiltless (Luke 23:41).

Together, those in high places, his contemporaries, disciples, apostles and customers proclaim his goodness. The verdict from them is the same: he spoke good words and performed great deeds. How did Jesus react to them? **How did he see himself?** When the disciples of John the Baptist asked who he was, he gave them an account of his personal effectiveness. His credentials were beyond question: "And he answered them, 'Go and tell John what you have seen and heard'" Luke 7: 22. There was nothing to hide. In explaining his role he likens himself to a shepherd, a metaphor easily understood by the crowd: "I am the Good Shepherd. The Good Shepherd lays down his life for his sheep" John 10:11.

The connection with his Mission Statement is too obvious

The Golden Rule

to escape attention. As part of his mission he had come to serve his fellow men; that he would accomplish. To make that possible, he made himself accessible to the common folk. People were happy to meet him and invite him over. He went graciously. And returned their hospitality when he had them over (especially the poor), to share his meager rations, consistent with the recommendation he made: "When you give a banquet, invite the poor, the crippled, the lame, and the blind. And you will be blessed, because they cannot repay you" Luke 14:13-14.

How often have we not known of ideas that would not blossom, products that would not be made, careers that would not take off, and companies that would not join the Big League, all because of a crippling malady, we call 'fear of failure'? Jesus did not suffer from this paralyzing affliction. He performed because of his strong beliefs. He performed despite his detractors. He performed because of his overflowing compassion. He loved deeply. And his love found expression in different ways.

What any leader would love to hear, what any professional would want on his appraisal form, came to Jesus unsolicited - from his customers: "They were astounded beyond measure, saying, 'He has done everything well'" Mark 7:37

Chapter 11
Sink or Sail Together

"For they can conquer, who believe they can."

~ Virgil.

Tuesday was another fast-paced day. At Alex's desk his cell phone had been buzzing right through the day. It was 5 o'clock and it buzzed again. Irked, Alex picked it up, planning to dismiss the caller abruptly. It was Victor on the line. Alex's mood changed instantly.

Victor: "How busy are you this evening?"

Alex: "Why? Tell me."

Victor: "Can you set aside an hour?"

Alex: "Yes."

Victor: "If that is okay by you. Tell Joseph to take your car home. Be my guest. I'll give you a drop home."

Alex: "Is there anything in particular that you wish to

discuss?"

    Victor: "Yes. You and I need to chat for a while."

    Alex: "I'll be ready at 5-55. Would that suit you?"

    Victor: "Fine."

Alex wondered what could be the problem, as he settled back in his chair. What was the 'chat' about? Could it be his appraisal? Or was someone back-stabbing? He put such thoughts aside, dispatched Sheila home at 5-30 and hung on, going through statements that would be discussed at the Regional Managers Meet scheduled for Thursday and Friday.

Victor looked in at 5:55 and they stepped out together. Nothing was said as they went down to the car park. Victor held the car door open for Alex, then took the wheel and eased his white Audi out of the car park; and still there was no small talk. Victor drove slowly and hummed a tune that Alex could not recognize. Alex looked at him for a hint, but there was none. They pulled up at the parking lot near the beach; stepped out and began walking towards the University Campus. Alex was waiting for a clue. What was Victor up to? To put an end to the tension, Alex asked:

Chapter 11 | Sink or Sail Together

"Victor, what did you have in mind?"

"Alex, I am glad you asked. I thought you never would." He paused for a while and continued. "I found you rather withdrawn on Sunday. Apathetic would be strong; perhaps aloof and disinterested would be more appropriate. The others were involved. You were not. Why?"

"Are you suggesting that I was not a caring host?"

"You know what I mean. We spent time discussing Jesus and you seemed distant. Why?"

"Perhaps, I had very little to contribute."

"Tell that to the marines. I know you well enough for that. Something was wrong."

"I was not in my usual form, perhaps."

"Don't kid me."

"Victor, this discussion on Jesus makes me very uncomfortable."

"Why? Of all people you to be uncomfortable with Jesus?"

"No. It is not that I am uncomfortable with Jesus. It is

The Golden Rule

just that I cannot see him in our situation. I cannot think of him being dragged into our corporate world. What do we have except pretensions, deceit, the chasing of money and fame and driving people to achieve our money goals? We are crazed with sales and more sales, profits and more profits. Jesus is God. I cannot have him mixed up with the corporate world. No."

"Let me try to understand you. You believe Jesus is God. I respect that. I shall not challenge your belief. I am not averse to studying that part of Jesus. You know that my wife also sees Jesus as God. Be assured that we are not assaulting or assailing his Divine Personality. I made that clear at the start. As a Christian you see his Divinity. As a human I see his person and his sterling qualities. Is that wrong? We are not into confusing the two parts. If you fear that, fear no more. None of us would confuse the two facets of his being or question any Divine attribute. What then do you fear?"

"Victor, try to understand me. From my early childhood, my mother taught me to love and respect Jesus, as my God. I have accepted him as God, and he will stay that way. I cannot tamper with that belief. I cannot change my mind-set."

Chapter 11 | Sink or Sail Together

"For heaven's sake, Alex, be reasonable. Who is suggesting that you change your mind-set? All that we are saying is look at the man, the person. Is there something for us to learn from that person? Surely you cannot put that down to sacrilege or blasphemy?"

"Victor, we have people like Jack Welch, Bill Gates and our own Ratan Tata. Let us try to figure out what kind of models they are. Let us learn from them."

"We shall do that, Alex. Have no doubts. As professionals we shall look everywhere to find answers to our questions. That very approach takes us to Jesus. Perhaps Jesus has different lessons to teach us. Not the ones that Jack Welch and Bill Gates have."

"Victor, is this really necessary? To me it is a traumatic experience. It is like combining the sublime with the sordid. Our corporate world leaves much to be desired."

"Precisely; for that very reason we need models that will help us change. Improve. And that can come only from models that transcend our petty lapses and grave indiscretions. We need to study the Gospels to find Jesus the model; a towering model."

The Golden Rule

"Are you suggesting that we can find no other model? No other person to follow?"

"No. I do not know enough to say that. But I see a strong option in Jesus. Frankly, at any time during our discussions did we show disrespect to the person of Jesus? Andy said that the High Priests were not among his admirers. And Sammy said that some of his customers tried to trap him in discourse. But for those remarks I found nothing offending. Even those comments were made not to offend, but to state the obvious."

"I am not accusing anyone of showing disrespect. No. I am just uncomfortable with the idea."

"Why did you agree to host the meeting at your home, when you had such reservations?"

"Remember, I told you I am a team-man. The need of my team comes first. Despite my discomfort with the subject, I put the interest of the team ahead of my feelings."

An uneasy pause followed. They walked for some distance without speaking a word, until Victor asked: "Alex, have you spoken with Susan?"

Chapter 11 | Sink or Sail Together

"Not yet."

"Why don't you? Perhaps she has something to say. And I am ready to listen."

"I'll do that."

"Will you do me two favors?"

"Yes I will."

" Talk to Susan tonight. Tell me about it tomorrow morning. Also, since you believe that Jesus is God, raise your heart to him. Talk to him. Tell him what we are about. Then get back to me. Could you do me these favors?"

"Certainly I shall."

"Like the night watchman who expectantly waits for the break of dawn, I am going to wait for your reply". Quoting from Scripture, Victor could not have concluded more appropriately.

They stopped at the soft drink parlor and grabbed two cans. As they walked back to the car finishing the drink, Alex seemed a little less stressed and Victor intuitively knew that Susan his wife, and Jesus, his God would resolve his doubts.

On Wednesday morning, Victor was in his office early;

The Golden Rule

even before Maya. He had to plan for his trip to Singapore on Sunday and prepare points for his interaction with the Marketing Managers and Regional Managers during their conference scheduled for Thursday and Friday. He had some mails to be checked and find ways of getting his VPs together for the 'idea' launch during the conference. There was much to be done, he thought. Maya barged in and was surprised to see the boss in his office earlier than usual. She asked if she could help, and came back with his usual coffee.

"Maya, I am sure you have lined up things for my Singapore Trip. Just go over all the arrangements. And if VP Marketing calls, put him on to me, no matter what I am doing."

Victor was alone with his thoughts. Deepak met him at home, late on Monday night to brief him on the work he had done; which was a lot. After meeting each of the VPs separately, during the day on Monday, he had put sense into many of the general observations and statements they made, tying up loose ends. He had handled the whole exercise splendidly. What would we do without Deepak? Even as Victor was lost in his thoughts, Maya tiptoed in.

Chapter 11 | Sink or Sail Together

"VP Marketing is waiting to meet you. Could he come in?"

"Of course, send him in immediately."

Alex walked in. The gray stripes on his maroon tie, against his light gray shirt, looked striking. Tall, handsome, well dressed, this fellow could make a lot of heads turn, Victor thought. He grabbed Alex by the hand and motioned him to a chair.

"Susan and I talked. I also prayed."

"Good. Thank you." Victor waited expectantly.

"There is some sense in what she says." There was a pause. And Victor did not break it.

"She says that I have to look beyond what I am doing now. Put simply, she says that the more depraved the situation, the greater the need for a loftier model. Since the sins of the corporate world would return to haunt us, we need a towering personality, an unmatched and powerful model, to exorcize those demons. Despite some great ones, most men have feet of clay. They would be imperfect models. After all, it is only the great personality of Jesus that we are examining. Not his Divinity. Come to think of it, his qualities are unmatched. He is peerless in forging and strengthening relationships. I did not sleep well. I kept thinking of what you had to say. Of what Susan had to say. And I prayed; again and again. Lead kindly light. Lead on, I asked. It was only after three this morning that I dozed off. I felt a lot better this morning. I thought I should not keep you in suspense. That is why I gate-crashed. Sorry I did not call you before coming."

Victor put up his hand to stop any further expressions of regret.

"Victor, I guess I was a little closed to the idea. I am sorry, I put you to distress. But the good thing is that we discussed it. You did not leave me wallowing in my own thoughts. I am glad you challenged me."

Victor sensed that Alex had been through a harrowing night, which explained his disjointed statements. But he understood Alex's predicament and captured the essence of his rambling conversation. Thankfully the crux made sense. He did not tell him that he had voiced the same thoughts that Susan had; only that he did it before she could express them. No; that was not his style.

"Alex, the watchman's vigil is over. And I have not

Chapter 11 | Sink or Sail Together

watched in vain. The break of dawn has brought me good news. Thank you. I was beginning to worry. What if you turned out to be the lone voice against the idea? I was counting on your support. And you were shooting off at a tangent. You know that with us it is simply, sink or sail together. I was puzzled. Deepak has done a great job putting things together. But we would have been beaten before we began, if you were not with us. Imagine talking to the Marketing Managers and Regional Managers without the support of their VP?"

"Yes, I can imagine that." Alex was sheepish.

"All's well that ends well." Victor was joyous.

"What next?" Alex asked.

"Friday's concluding session, it will be. You had invited Mr Das, our consultant, to address your team. We shall cancel that and give him an opportunity some other time. This Friday afternoon it will be in-house inputs. Deepak will handle the session with your active support. I'll just kick start it. Remember Jesus said that a good tree does not bear bad fruit. Ours is a good tree - a great idea. Let us taste the feedback fruit that our managers give us on Friday afternoon."

The Golden Rule

Chapter 12
The Need to Change

"I want to change things. I want to see things happen. I don't want just to talk about them."

~ J.K. Galbraith

After much preparation by the presenters and great anticipation in the participants, the special session was to start at about 2:05 pm on Friday. Victor Banerjee, the Chief Executive, walked into the Conference Hall. A sudden hush fell over the group of managers assembled for their review meeting. For a day and a half they labored over figures and strategies; over tactics and promotional offers. This afternoon it would be different. They would introspect, as people, as professionals, on ideas removed from targets and deadlines.

Seated around the conference table, in the Summit Room, were Deepak Chopra, Alex Thomas, Andy Kelkar, Sammy Ghosh, and Gaps Iyer, the five Vice Presidents, Rahul Mathew, Sunil

The Golden Rule

Vachani, Lokesh Mishra, the three Marketing Managers, reporting to Alex Thomas, and Latif Basha, Mahesh Kaul, Deb Mukerjee, Satish Lobo, Muthukrishnan and Ms Kiran Desai, the six Regional Managers, reporting to the Marketing Managers. India was divided into five regions. The sixth Regional Manager oversaw exports. With the rest of the world seen as a region, Ms Kiran Desai also was designated as Regional Manager, with a suffix, `Export'. The export activity was not big. But there were hopes of enlarging the scale of operations. (Not all these managers attended business school; some moved up to their current positions, working their way up from field jobs in Sales. Many were savvy in their functions, but were not abreast of management thinking. This afternoon the top team hoped to bridge the gap a little). With the Chief Executive there were 15 in the conference hall. This was a typical summit at Mount Pharmaceuticals.

The Chief Executive stood up, looked around and began rather slowly. "Gentlemen and Ms Desai, you are here for the customary Review Meeting. The Vice President, Marketing, and you have interacted. I have no doubts that you have had a rewarding day-and-a-half of such deliberations. Later, I shall discuss the meeting with Mr. Alex Thomas. Now I shall not touch

Chapter 12 | The Need to Change

on any of the points already covered. I am here for a different purpose. I said that you are here for the customary Review Meeting. I must correct myself. It is not customary. It should not be customary. Each should be special; different. This meeting I assure you will be different. The Vice Presidents and I have discussed a few new ideas. We would like to have your initial response to these ideas. Vice President, Human Resources, Mr. Deepak Chopra, will place these ideas before the house. Your boss, Mr. Thomas, will step in where necessary. So will the other Vice Presidents. I am here just to let you know that the afternoon session is of tremendous importance to you and to your company. Please discuss the ideas with an open mind. Feel free to sound your reservations, if you have any. But please be plain. Do realize that we value your opinions. That is the reason we planned this session. I shall leave now. But I shall return before you conclude. I wish you a fruitful discussion. Thank you." There was silence as he left the conference room.

    Deepak Chopra moved to the top of the table. Behind him was the screen for his power point presentation and to his right, the white board, on which he would write down some points. He smiled warmly at his audience; ensured that eye contact was right

The Golden Rule

and began. "Gentlemen and Ms Desai, I welcome you to an afternoon of idea-storming. Did you notice that the Chief and I addressed the gentlemen before the lady? It is just because of the larger number of men in this room; no offense is meant to the lady. On purpose I do not call it brain-storming, because we shall be breaking the conventional rules of brain-storming. With the Chief, I wish you an enjoyable afternoon.

Let me begin this afternoon's session with a little story. It is an adapted version of a legend, used by Shiv Khera in one of his books. The words spoken by the characters in the story are mine.

The wise old man of a village is sitting under a big tree. It is early afternoon. A traveler stops by and addresses the old man.

`Uncle, could you tell me about the people of your village?'

`Why would you want to know that?' The old man enquires.

`I am having trouble at my village. I wish to move out to another village. And find some work to do', the stranger replies.

`I shall certainly tell you about the people in this village. But first, will you tell me about the people in your village?' The old man's experience shows.

Chapter 12 | The Need to Change

'The less said the better. The people in my village are rude, mean, quarrelsome and foul-mouthed. They are evil!' he hisses.

'Sadly, the people in this village are the same. They are evil'. As he said this, the old man looked pensive. The stranger shook his head and moved on.

The next afternoon the old man is again at his favorite spot.

Another traveler stops and asks him: `Uncle, could you please advise me? I want to shift out of my village to another village. I do not have much work, where I am. I am trying to find a village where I can get some work and where people are kind. Are people in this village kind?'

The old man says: `Tell me about the people in your village'.

`Oh! They are just wonderful; so helpful. They do not want me to move out. But unless I find work, my family will starve. The people will help me. I have no doubt. But I cannot accept help every day. So I must find work in a new place, where I am welcome'.

The old man is silent for a long time. Then he says: `Finding work here is not going to be difficult. We have farms who hire hands. And as for people here, they are wonderful, very helpful'. The stranger smiles, thanks the old man, and promises to return. That is the end of the story."

Deepak looked around. He noticed that his audience was trying to grapple with the different responses of the old man.

"What do you think is the moral of the story?" Deepak questioned.

Satish, eager to participate, ventured: "Good and bad are relative. There are no absolutes."

"Can you explain that?" Deepak pushed.

"What he meant to say was: If you look through colored glasses you see things colored." Ms Kiran Desai interrupted.

"Thank you, Kiran, but let him try to explain," Deepak urged.

"Kiran spoke well," Satish promptly agreed with his colleague.

"I think this is a clear case of perceptions. How perceptions are different and how they matter," Sunil pointed out.

Chapter 12 | The Need to Change

"Are you trying to say that we see things not the way they are, but the way we are? The first traveler thought evil. And he found evil. The second traveler looked for good. And he found good. Was the old man trying to say that if you look at people with fellow-feeling you will find friendship? Looking at things with clear eyes and looking at things with jaundiced eyes make a difference!"

"Well said", Sunil complimented Deepak.

"Thank you, Sunil, you are kind", Deepak said and continued: "Are we agreed on the moral of the story?" There were reaffirming nods.

"Let me ask you a question: In our context, who is a professional? What is our perception of one?" There was a twinkle in Deepak's eyes as he placed the posers before them. There was silence since they were afraid to say anything stupid.

Lokesh broke the silence: "In very simple terms, a professional is one who manages the resources he has. These could be products, markets, trade, cash and people; just anything. He tries to maximize returns from these resources."

Deepak looked at him approvingly, and said: "You could say that. There are several definitions in management books. We are not going to spend our time discussing those. We are not writing examinations or appearing for interviews. What we want to examine are, our perceptions."

Now that Lokesh had spoken his mind, others followed with Rahul coming in next: "I think Lokesh gave us the crux. I might want to change the term maximize to effectively manage."

"So you say that the word maximize has its hidden dangers. Effective management is a happy blend of all kinds of effort," Deepak suggested.

"Yes. When you want to maximize results from one resource, the results from another could get compromised. Effective management would mean, balancing." Rahul explained.

"'Management is therefore not a matter of answers or solutions but a precarious balancing act.' Those are the words of Stuart Grainer who writes in Business, the Jack Welch Way," Gaps added.

"To do this balancing act, the professional must have knowledge and skills", Mahesh elaborated.

"What about his attitudes and beliefs?" Latif challenged,

and added, "A study done at Harvard University showed that 85 per cent of the time, a person gets a job or a promotion because of his attitude, and only 15 percent on account of his educational qualification and skill."

Deepak took the cue and amplified: "Shiv Khera is reported to have said that his interactions with Chief Executives in different parts of the world have thrown up one factor - Attitude. They tell him that, the most important factor that affects productivity, profits, and team work, is attitude".

Latif was elated with the support he got from Deepak Chopra, and conveyed his appreciation.

"A professional must effectively manage the resources he has or procures. To do that, he must have the requisite knowledge, skills, habits and attitude. Would we be right in proposing that?" Deepak looked askance.

Both Deb and Kiran started out at once. But Deb managed to get it across: "To me, that seems fine. But the conditions in which he operates will help or hinder progress. For example, if he works for a company where there is suspicion, or lack of encouragement, then his performance could suffer despite the other strong points."

"I agree with Deb," Kiran echoed.

"So a professional must learn to cope with circumstances that are apparently not in his control?" Deepak looked at Deb and Kiran.

Muthukrishnan did not like being left out: "How can he manage things outside his control?"

"Correct me, if I am wrong, but I recall suggesting that a manager must learn to cope with, and not manage, factors outside his control", Deepak clarified.

"He must have the resilience to cope with several pressures: task-generated, people-generated and situation-generated," Kiran expanded. And she knew what she was saying, because in the export market the pressures she had to cope with were often outside her control.

"In other words his attitudes would cover a wide range, including the attitude of coping with such situations." Lokesh intoned.

"Why are you leaving out his knowledge and skills?"

Chapter 12 | The Need to Change

Mahesh questioned.

"Please yourself. Have them all". Lokesh smiled.

"Why not one of you summarize the points we have just covered?" Deepak requested.

Rahul looked around, "May I?" he asked. There were approving smiles. "A professional is first a person. He must never forget that. He has his limitations. So he must not stop learning. To learn he must be open. To effectively manage his resources, which could be big and diverse, or small and limited, he must have adequate knowledge. And constantly upgrade his knowledge. He must have good work habits - like being organized and systematic. He must be positive, optimistic, friendly, keep the good of the company above all else, respect people, have no double standards and possess skills of a high order; like communication and interpersonal skills. These should be far above average". There was spontaneous applause when he finished.

"Rahul, you spoke well. I liked your clarity of thought". Deepak commended, and quickly put up a slide, adding that he got the slide at a seminar he attended, and was not sure of the source.

The Golden Rule

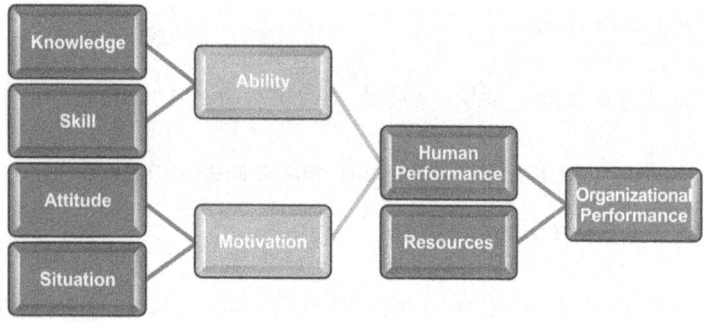

"What Rahul was trying to tell us is summed up in this slide", Deepak said, even as he saw the participants busily writing down what they just read on the slide. "I would like to add that he is seen as a competent professional when he does his job well. But that is half the story. Unless he learns to interact successfully with those in his team and those outside, his competence is dented. He will have to learn to perform well on his own and raise the level of team-performance to ensure a high standard of achievement. Starting and sustaining happy relationships is a professional quality that goes at a premium. Most of us are still learning how to do it. We shall discuss this point a little later."

"Now that we have some thoughts on the subject, we shall put it on hold for a while. I promise you, we shall return to it." Deepak seemed anxious to move on.

Chapter 12 | The Need to Change

"You recall we said that perceptions matter. And those perceptions color our thinking. So to change ourselves, we must change our perceptions. Would that be a fair conclusion?" Deepak looked for response. There was overall approval.

"The question to my mind is: should we change at all? Why not continue the way we are? Are there compelling reasons for us to change?" Deepak challenged.

Latif who had been silent for some time, took up the challenge: "I believe that change is the only thing that is certain because every facet of life changes. We are not what we were last year. Hopefully we shall not be what we are now, next year. Change we must, of that I am certain."

"If change is a must, as Latif eloquently explained, then we must ask ourselves, where we stand today, to decide in what areas we need to change. One tool that helps us do that, is our Appraisal. We are familiar with the tool we use now. The question is: Is the Appraisal, the way we do it now, appropriate?" Deepak let the question sink.

"For now, we have our boss do the appraisal with us. Do you say that is not complete?" Deb demanded.

"I am not saying so. I am asking the house. Do we think it is adequate? Should we, for example, get to know what our peers have to say about us?" Deepak was testing the waters.

"How can our peers comment on us? Only the boss should." Deb, who had not been to business school, was emphatic.

"Don't we transact with our peers? Don't we have relationships with them? When the relationship is good, are we not able to gain their support in getting things done?" Deepak enquired.

"Yes. It helps. But are they to get involved in the appraisal?" Deb was anxious.

"Are we afraid of the consequences? Do we fear that our poor performances will get noticed even by our peers?" Deepak asked.

"Fear of a wrong interpretation by them is real." Muthukrishnan admitted.

"When the feedback is positive from peers, does it not add to our confidence?" Deepak angled.

"It does." Mahesh answered.

Chapter 12 | The Need to Change

"To ensure that we get positive feedback from our peers, we shall have to perform well. Perhaps change some of our ways. Pressure ourselves to change," Deepak deduced.

"You are coming around to the need for change," Kiran wised up.

"Precisely, we all have to change. We have to set ourselves high standards. And welcome feedback from our peers. Why, even from our subordinates and customers because we work with all of them; and we build relationships with them," Deepak extended the logic.

Deb wished to interrupt, but Deepak begged him to wait and continued, as he put up another slide.

"One writer sums up the idea in this way." He pointed to the slide.

"Perhaps, what he meant was that we do not manage a company. We manage people. Mr. Godrej, the noted Indian Industrialist, echoed the same thought when he said: 'All corporate strengths are dependent on people'."

The Golden Rule

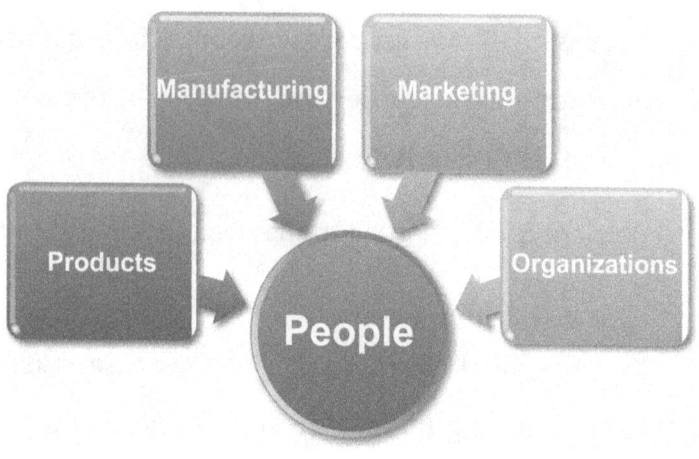

Then turning to Deb he said: "Deb, did you wish to say something?"

"Subordinates; no way; how can we let our subordinates appraise us? The idea is preposterous." Deb was indignant and loud.

"Would you like to be told that your subordinates think well of you; that you are fair-minded; that you set the right example; and so on?" Deepak pitched.

"Yes. I would love to hear that, but not through an Appraisal", Deb defended.

"Why? Are we terrified at the prospect? Take a look at our

Chapter 12 | The Need to Change

interactions in our work situations. We are interacting with a network of seniors, juniors, peers and external Agencies, like Customers, Suppliers, Traders, Advertising Agencies, Transporters, Bankers and others. And the nature of our interactions determines the success of those interactions. When we interact well, we build good relationships. And good relationships help in good performance. Can you fault that logic?" Deepak contended.

Deepak put up another slide.

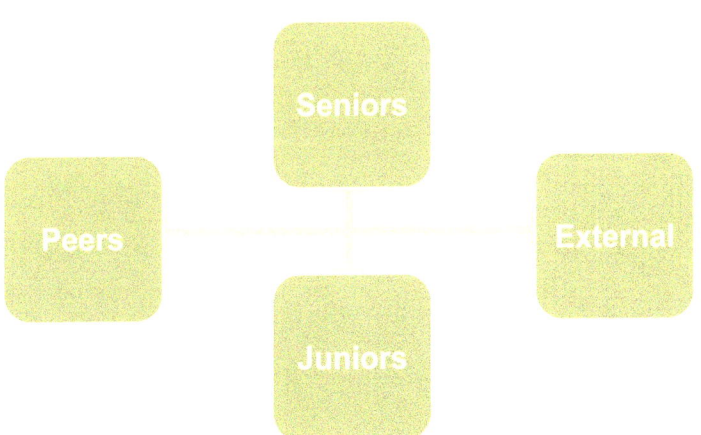

"A performing professional should not have fears. He knows what he has to do; and does it. The opinions of others should interest him. Not disturb him. Chances are that those opinions will be positive, because he is a performing professional". Alex spoke for the first time. So far it was only the VP Human Resources who engaged them in discussion. Now it was their Head who was speaking. They listened intently. There was finality to his words.

"Since we are performing professionals, we have little to fear from any source. Only those who are non-performing are weighed down by such fears. For us, the boss, the peer, the subordinate, or even the customer, should have good things to say, because we perform." Deepak reinforced what Alex said.

"In a way, what you say is right. I suppose it is just the resistance to change, inherent in us. The gate of change can be opened only from the inside. And right now we are reluctant to open that gate." Lokesh confessed.

"We know that an Appraisal from different people can throw up some points we had not expected. The element of surprise; one is uncomfortable with that." Sunil gave another dimension to Lokesh's admission.

"Granted; your point is valid for the first time, the second time and perhaps the third time. But if we are focused on

Chapter 12 | The Need to Change

improvement, in time, these surprise elements will be behind us. We would have acted on them and improved to that extent. Has not the professional to be open to change, starting with himself? In the final analysis what we are, communicates far more eloquently than anything we say or do." Deepak, borrowing the idea from Stephen R. Covey, slid that in deftly.

"Mr. Chopra, could you please get to the point? You have teased us long enough." Rahul entreated. There was laughter all around.

"My intention was never to tease you, Rahul. It was only to draw you out; to gain consensus, if possible, for a new idea that I shall promptly propose to the house; since the ground work is done," Deepak explained. And continued: "Now that I have your attention, I wish to place before you the 360° Appraisal, a new tool in the Indian context." With that he had a new slide in place. The slide showed four quadrants.

Some of them were acquainted with the tool through sessions in business school. The others, who had no management education, had questioning looks on their face, as they tried to figure out the illustration. Each was busy with his own thoughts.

The Golden Rule

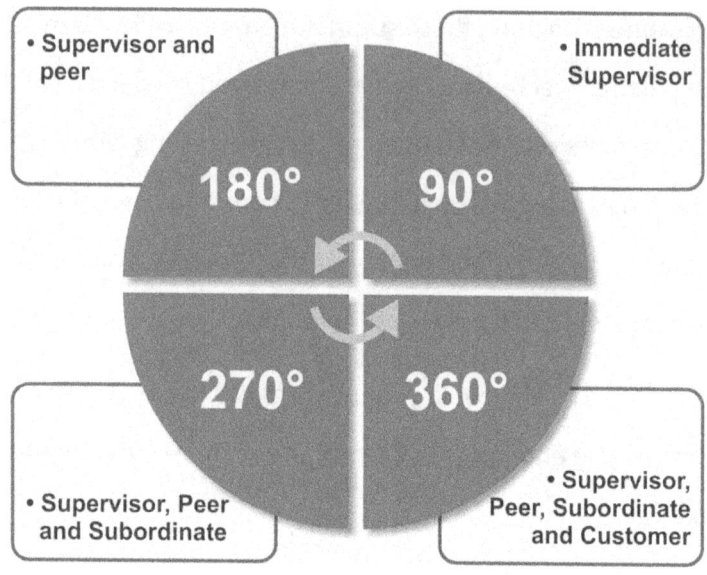

"As of now, we have only the 90° appraisal. Each of us is assessed by his immediate supervisor, with some comments from the boss of the immediate supervisor. For Regional Managers, we have the appraisal done by the Marketing Managers. The Vice President, Marketing, makes a few points in the appraisal form, if necessary. As a first step, we propose a planned shift to the 180° appraisal, when peers also will submit feedback on the one being assessed. For example, a Regional Manager will get his feedback from the other Regional Managers. This will give the appraisal a new dimension. In stages we shall move to the 270 degree, where subordinates are consulted, and finally to the 360 degree, where customer opinions are invited. The 360 degree appraisal will be the sum total of feedback from four segments.

The traditional method is subjective; often based on the equation between the individual and his or her immediate boss. In the new system, the boss is more like a judge. The multi-source feedback is like a jury looking at the means adopted by the individual to get results. The jury submits findings to the boss before the verdict is pronounced by him. He will continue to judge results and will remain the final authority. Here, he has a chance of checking other opinions, instead of relying only on his. Then he announces his verdict. By doing that, the system improves on the traditional method. It is also important to remember that the company looks for trends and patterns and not flashes of brilliance or outstanding performance in fits and starts. When we reach the 360° Appraisal in good time, some of the areas that will be spotlighted are: Vision, Pursuit of Excellence, Sense of Accountability, and the Extent of Empowerment, that we can bring to bear on our function. You will notice that these are some of the key qualities that top management value. So someone showing improving trends in these areas is well on his way up." Deepak

The Golden Rule

paused, watching carefully, for reactions. Nobody spoke. So he went on.

"Some other companies have gone ahead of us; we have been slow to change. It is time we caught up. First, we shall have to be educated on the 360° appraisal. How shall we give feedback; positive and negative? Have we to fear retribution when giving negative feedback? How objective should we be? We shall have to feel responsible for the feedback we give. We shall have to fix a number to those who will be involved in rating. Who will these be? What parameters will be used in giving feedback? We must know how to handle negative feedback and build on positive feedback. We have much to learn. We have no illusions. We will make mistakes in the learning process. In time, after pilot tests, we shall work out a system that reduces the losses and increases the gains."

He paused again, on purpose, yet there was no comment. And then he threw them the direct challenge: "Are we ready for such a change?" Some shifted in their chairs. Others looked away. The pause was long.

"How soon do you plan to start the new system?" Satish

Chapter 12 | The Need to Change

asked nervously.

"How soon do you think? Would the next appraisal be okay with you?" Deepak enquired.

"Okay by me", Mahesh declared.

"Me too," Kiran joined in. The rest looked at Mahesh and Kiran in askance.

"So we are agreed on two points: One, we introduce the 180° appraisal when the next appraisals are due. And two, we shall progressively move to the 270° and 360° appraisal based on the success we have with the 180°." Deepak wrapped it up.

"Yes. That should be fine, Mr. Chopra," Alex said. "And thank you. You had us keep on our thinking caps."

"Thank you Mr. Thomas." Deepak replied warmly.

Tea and short eats made the rounds as small groups got into conversation. A fifteen-minute break gave them a chance to stretch and compare notes; in hushed tones. The Chief was right. This was different.

The Golden Rule

Chapter 13

The Change Agent

"We are not human beings having a spiritual experience. We are spiritual beings having a human experience."

~ Teilhard de Chardin.

The afternoon session had set minds racing. New systems were in the offing that did not appeal to them. How were they going to fend off negative feedback in the appraisal system? What would happen if the feedback was damaging? Could peers be trusted to give favorable remarks? There were too many thoughts crowding their minds and too little time to address them. So, they decided to reassemble for the session after tea, a little agitated, yet curious to know if more upsetting news was in store for them. It was just past 3-40. As Deepak Chopra stood up again, looking fresh after a wash, they sensed that more serious stuff was to follow.

"Gentlemen and Ms Desai, I must thank you for your

The Golden Rule

undivided attention in the pre-tea session. I urge you to think with me in the post-tea session. It should be equally momentous," Deepak exhorted them, by way of an introduction, and continued: "You recall Rahul summarizing for us what he thought, a professional should be. Let us put down the points." So saying, he began to write on the white board.

A Professional should be:

1. A person,
2. Open,
3. Prepared to learn continually,
4. Able to effectively manage resources,
5. Ready to improve his knowledge,
6. Organized and systematic,
7. Positive, optimistic and friendly,
8. Conscious that his company is above all else,
9. Respectful of people,
10. Free of double-standards,
11. Good at Communicating and

Chapter 13 | The Change Agent

12. Good in his interpersonal skills.

Looking directly at Rahul he said: "That was fairly comprehensive Rahul. Do accept my compliments".

"Thank you, Mr. Chopra, you make my day." Rahul returned the compliment.

"Has anyone to add points to the list?" Deepak asked.

"Broadly that covers some of a professional's attitudes, skills, knowledge, and work habits. But I am not sure if the list is complete." Sunil's rather lame statement did not help.

"The list can never be complete. One can always go on adding points to the list. We are looking at the essentials," Kiran proposed.

"For now, we'll put the list on hold and come back to it in time. We shall make a small departure to look for names of people who are good professionals, based on what we have learned so far; those we can learn from. Can you name a few?" Deepak shot off at a tangent.

"Jack Welch," Lokesh suggested.

"Ratan Tata," Satish added.

The Golden Rule

"Definitely, these people are seen as successful Professionals. And we have much to learn from them," Deepak agreed. "Can you think of them as models?" he questioned.

"Yes and no," Mahesh puzzled. "Yes in the sense that they have much to teach us; no in the sense that they are far from being perfect. They too stumble and fall."

"Put differently, what we need is a model that is definitely far above the rest of us," Deepak extrapolated.

"Yes; very definitely." Alex affirmed. All eyes turned to him.

"Let us try and put down the qualities that a super model should have; focusing on people skills. We already said that a professional manages not a company, but people. Therefore we should focus on qualities that help build relationships," Deepak led them on and put up a slide.

	Team Person
1	He sets criteria for team selection
2	He has a flat structure, to have ready access to his teammates
3	He gives them a goal; a mission; and focus
4	He continually teaches the team

5	He encourages and motivates the team
6	He defends the team against adversaries
7	He chides them when he must
8	He overrules them when he should
9	He identifies himself with them
10	He delegates
11	He creates trust and confidence. The team believes in him and accepts him
12	He enjoys their obedience and affection
13	He names and trains his successor

Notes were made, as the slide was on. The next slide came up.

People Person	
1	He has empathy for people.
2	He is not patronizing or condescending.
3	He follows the open door policy.
4	He sets an example through good conduct.
5	He shuns popularity. Only focuses on the task; the Mission.
6	He does not wallow in self-pity, in tribulation.
7	He is humble (a tree laden with fruit, bends low).

The Golden Rule

8	He forgives readily and does not remind the offender of his wrong-doing.
9	He is generous in his praise of others. He compliments readily.
10	He is fair and open and has no favorites; no double standards.
11	He rewards generously.
12	He takes the rough with the smooth; with composure.
13	He can almost read the thoughts of people around him. He can dipstick their motives.
14	He takes the initiative, in building a relationship. Especially with those who are timid.
15	He holds himself accountable and expects accountability from others.
16	He has a vision, which he shares with others.
17	He pursues that vision with zest.
18	He handles conflicts with ease
19	He looks at the weakness of others with understanding, not accusation.
20	He hopes that his people will have faith and confidence in him.

When they had finished with this slide, the next came up.

	Skilled Person
1	He has analytical skills which combine well with imaginative and intuitive thinking.

2	He has conceptual and creative skills.
3	He has motivating and problem-solving skills.
4	He has interpersonal skills to sustain successful transactions.
5	He has communication skills of a high order.
6	He has planning and organizing skills in good measure.
7	He has time management skills that earn him praise.
8	He has skills to co-ordinate money, material and infrastructure.
9	He has skills to perform consistently, edifying teams and improving performance.

After putting up the 3 slides Deepak stopped. He shut his laptop and looked at his audience very intently. They were looking up from their pads, even as they finished making notes, but no one spoke. "I owe Ms Desai an explanation: 'He' in our discussions does not exclude a 'she'. There is no gender bias. A lady can be the professional we are discussing. I hope I am clear, Ms Desai?" She gave him an understanding smile.

"Should a professional be concerned only with building brands, market penetration and share, creation of assets, financial ratios, and stakeholder returns? Can he perform outside of these parameters?" Deepak's searching question, had them looking at each other.

"We are accustomed to thinking of professionals operating under such compulsions, that it is difficult to visualize anyone operating outside those parameters." Lokesh said feebly.

"For example, could a professor, a teacher, be considered a professional? Would a pastor or a preacher be called one?" Deepak demanded.

"Not in our context", Sunil ventured.

"Why?" Andy, speaking for the first time, questioned.

"Maybe, that is our mindset." Sunil replied.

"Since we are on the subject of change, should we not change our mindsets and consider the basic profile of the professional? He is one who effectively manages resources," Gaps argued.

"If we stretch it, 'yes' would be the answer," Sunil conceded.

"In which case, people like Mahatma Gandhi, Martin

Luther King Jr. and Mother Teresa, were professionals?" Gaps persisted.

"In a way, yes," Sunil agreed.

"Good. So we are not stuck with people like Jack Welch or Bill Gates or Ratan Tata", Deepak checked.

"No, we can look beyond them," Sunil generously complied.

"In which case, the list of traits, qualities, that we put up for a super model could serve as a guideline; even if that model is not Steve Jobs," Deepak was trying hard to connect.

"Someone who has those qualities is certainly bigger than he is," Kiran stated emphatically.

"Could you think of someone who can fit the frame?" Rahul asked.

"Yes." Deepak now knew he could hold out no longer. The climax was at hand.

"And who could that be?" Rahul checked.

"**Jesus Christ**!" Deepak declared.

The Golden Rule

Satish almost jumped off his chair and promptly looked at Rahul and then at Alex, the other Christians in the room. Alex and Rahul were unruffled. How can these people be doing this? But he chose to remain silent. Latif was not amused. He looked angry. The others looked around to check reactions. They were amused at first, assuming that Deepak was joking. Then they turned grim when they found that he was serious.

"He is not a professional. He is a religious leader!" Latif sounded very provoked.

"That he was a religious leader is certain. Why can't he be a professional? Did he not effectively manage his resources?" Deepak contended.

"In which case, why not call the prophet of Islam, a model professional?" Latif was incensed.

"You have a point there," Deepak affirmed. "He too can be a Model-Professional. We have not studied his background. We have studied the background of Jesus."

"So, even Lord Krishna can be treated as a Model-Professional?" Muthukrishnan questioned.

Chapter 13 | The Change Agent

"Yes. We are not averse to examining anyone. We chanced to study the life and teachings of Jesus. We find enough reason to put him up as a model," Deepak explained.

"But we know nothing of him," Kiran argued.

"You know nothing of him or very little of him, now. But you can get to know him if you have an open mind. We believe that as professionals we have open minds," Gaps took up issue, recalling his own closed responses when Victor brought it up the first time.

"As professionals we are supposed to have open minds," Deb stated matter-of-factly.

"Not supposed to have, but should have," Gaps corrected.

"So, with an open mind, we can look at the life and operations of Jesus. Not in the religions sense. Not to agree with our Christian teammates, but to find in Jesus a professional whom we can set up as a model. To help you do that, we have for you copies of the New Testament and additional reading material. Once you have studied that, you will see what we have seen," Deepak entreated.

The Golden Rule

He paused and asked: "Are we agreed on the action?"

They nodded, but not with much conviction. They had the odd feeling that they were being rushed into something.

Victor walked in as Deepak was finishing.

"How is it going?" he asked.

"They were confused and disturbed at first; now they are ready to investigate, rather grudgingly." Deepak summed up.

Victor rose and surveyed his team. Good performers, by and large; young expectant faces. The future of the company lay in their hands. The company needed them and counted on them. It was important that they understood and accepted ideas. No change would be possible otherwise.

"Gentlemen and Ms Desai" he started, "Perhaps you wonder why your counterparts from the other departments are not here this afternoon; especially when you are trying to understand ideas that could affect us all. You are in touch with our customers; in touch with the market. Your responses are important; very important. Not that the responses of the others are not important. But because you interact with customers, your response must be had first. In the fourth quadrant of the 360° Appraisal, we are to seek feedback from customers. That should explain it. Without customers, good and loyal customers there will be no company. And without marketing we would not be reaching those customers. Anything that we do internally must translate into customer benefits. And you are the best judges of benefits that should reach our customers. That is why we chose to speak with you first. Then we shall repeat the exercise with the other departments." He stopped, drank a few sips of water and looked at his audience to pick up signals. There were mixed signals – anticipation in some and disinterest in others. Then he continued.

"Mr. Deepak Chopra and the other Vice Presidents have tried, in the time available, to put across some ideas to you - different ideas; ideas that look strange. And yet they have not been placed before you without thought. The Vice Presidents and I have done much thinking, and debating. Mr. Chopra placed those ideas before you in capsule form. As pharmaceutical people you have many capsules in your product range; therefore you will understand the relevance. This capsule has two colors. The first color represents the 360° Appraisal that we plan to introduce in stages. We gather that General Electric initiated the use of the tool. Some Indian companies are trying to make it compatible with their operations. Reliance, Godrej, Wipro, and Infosys are some, I learn. When we join this select band we shall be in exalted company. The system is not without its demerits. What would these be?

First: there could be bias, of the person doing the rating; positive or negative.

Second: the one assessed may sense humiliation and find it difficult to accept negative feedback from many people.

Third: there are difficulties and limitations in linking such an appraisal with rewards, such as increments and promotions.

On the merit side, what do we have?

First: the management-style of the person is assessed - the methods he uses to achieve results. Some introspection normally follows such feedback. As a result, s/he could decide to pursue excellence, because of dividends guaranteed by improved performance.

Second: subtle pressure is experienced, to change, to improve, and to be accountable.

Chapter 13 | The Change Agent

Third: with so much feedback given, team work is likely to improve. Some solidarity with the team will follow.

Fourth: it could teach us to delegate better. We could understand what empowerment is all about.

And this is the test. Some of our hidden infirmities could get exposed. Some skeletons from the cupboard could fall out; much to our surprise. But since our intention is to use the tool for improvement, we should put the findings to good use.

Let me tell you what happened to Mr. Godrej, Chief Executive of Godrej. When the 360° Appraisal was introduced in his company, he set an example by being the first to be assessed. And to his surprise he discovered that his managers wanted him to be less authoritarian. He perceived himself differently. But here were managers telling him that he should change. Taking a cue from Mr. Godrej, I propose to be the first in our company to take the 180° Appraisal, when we introduce it, and do it first at the 270° stage and finally at the 360° stage. As you get to know the manner in which it will be administered, you will find that many of your fears are baseless. We are working on the project. Mr. Chopra hopes to be ready with 180° in about 4-6 weeks. We shall then

The Golden Rule

get back to you.

You recall I mentioned that the capsule has two colors. I said that one color represented the 360° appraisal system. It is obvious that the new appraisal system focuses on relationships. Broadly, our relationships are divided into two types: external and internal relationships. The external relationships are those that we build with people outside the company: Customers, Suppliers, Agents and so on. The internal relationships are built with seniors, peers, juniors and top management. The 360° tries to cover the spectrum. If you extend the reasoning, you find that life itself is a network of relationships. And the happy man is one who ensures good relationships with all: family, friends and associates. Our success in life depends largely on how we redefine our relationships with those who interact with us. Targeting relationships, we tried to find a model for ourselves. A model that would help us put relationships in perspective. Transform our relationships. Raise our standards. And give us the impetus to try harder. In short, empower us to become better human beings. We discovered Jesus Christ from the Gospels. We discovered him, not by design, but by accident. I chanced to read the Gospels. That is how I got acquainted with Jesus. With the little I gained by

Chapter 13 | The Change Agent

reading the Gospels, I persuaded the VPs to read them. Then, we decided to get more information on Jesus. After that, the Vice Presidents and I discussed our findings. We were overwhelmed. None of us wants you to imagine that there is a religious angle to this attempt. We looked at him only as a professional. We found outstanding qualities in him, and realized that there were very few contenders to match him. At least, from those we know. He is the answer to our questions. Now, we are not against examining other options. People who have stellar qualities like Jesus. It could be an ongoing process. And we are open to suggestions. For now, Jesus strikes us as a remarkable model. The other color in the capsule represents Jesus. The 360° appraisal is fulfilled in Jesus, the epitome of professional relationships; the change agent. I understand your difficulty. You have not met Jesus and made His acquaintance. You have your opportunity now. Mr. Chopra has given you copies of the New Testament and copies of reading material that the VPs and I have studied. I have a suggestion to offer. You could read the material and at least the Gospel of Mathew. We could meet on Sunday for a while, before you return to your offices. What do you say?"

"Let us not disturb their Sunday plans," Alex pleaded.

The Golden Rule

"Why not meet on Saturday afternoon?" Deepak asked.

"Will they be able to finish reading the material?" Victor enquired.

"I should think so, if they set aside a few hours tonight and a few hours tomorrow," Gaps worked out.

"Well then, at 4:05 tomorrow, we meet. I promise you that we shall not keep you beyond two hours. If we stay later, it will be because you want it." Now that the conference was officially over, they wanted to move out. Victor sensed that and said: "We shall say goodnight now. As you leave, please collect from Mr. Chopra copies of two more articles titled: The Communicator and Leadership and Change. This will be in addition to the other reading material he gave you. We shall look forward to seeing you tomorrow after you have made your acquaintance with Jesus."

Chapter 14
The Communicator

"The person who is eloquent of speech and unafraid of the assembly is hard to defeat in debate."

~ The Indian Poet, Thiruvalluvar (Verse 647)

One of the many reasons Jesus was special, was that he had strong skills. One of them was his fine-tuned ability to touch the heads and hearts of people with inspiring thoughts and well chosen words. Therefore, his powerful communication skills are placed alongside his magnetic personality and charisma. Jesus wrote nothing. He spoke mostly in Aramaic, a Hebrew dialect. So, only his verbal communication is assessed. Strangely, even his silences spoke effectively. The high priests and Pilate, the Governor, discovered how potent his silence was.

The Gospels use different words (amazed, astonished, astounded, spellbound) to convey the impact Jesus had on his listeners. Experts, down the centuries, equally convinced, have extolled his unmatched communication skills. To gain such a place, he certainly used tools and techniques that have been the envy of many. What were these? How did he employ them; with what distinction?

1) As a gifted **story teller**, Jesus used the Parable as one of the more effective tools (Matt 13:34). Parables are stories of human interest in the social, political and economic context. Farms and farm life, merchants and commerce, noblemen and servants, the temple and devotees, the law and its practice, feasts and festivals were nuggets for his stories. These compact stories with a moral helped preserve the message. Years later, as people reflected on what Jesus taught, his parables came to mind in vivid detail. Some writers refer to these parables as earthly stories with a heavenly intent. The stories he told were simple, direct and very compelling like, the Prodigal Son (considered to be the perfect short story), the Lost Sheep, the Lost Coin and the Good Samaritan which have not lost their relevance despite several repetitions down the ages.

The timeless parable of the Good Samaritan proves the point that he used such stories to good effect: "Just then a lawyer stood up to test Jesus. 'Teacher', he said, 'What must I do to inherit eternal life?' He said to him, 'What is written in the law? What do you read there?' He answered, 'You shall love the lord your God with all your heart and with all your soul and with all your strength and with all your mind, and your neighbor as yourself'. And he said to him, 'you have given the right answer; do this, and you will live'. But wanting to justify himself, he asked Jesus, 'And who is my neighbor?' Jesus replied, 'A man was going down from Jerusalem to Jericho, and fell into the hands of robbers, who stripped him, beat him, and went away, leaving him half dead. Now by chance a priest was going down that road; and when he saw him, he passed by on the other side. So likewise a Levite, when he came to the place and saw him, passed by on the other side. But a Samaritan while traveling came near him; and when he saw him, he was moved with pity. He went to him and bandaged his wounds, having poured oil and wine on them. Then he put him on his own animal, brought him to an inn, and took care of him. The next day he took out two denarii, gave them to the inn keeper, and said, 'Take care of him; and when I come back, I will repay you whatever more you spend'. Which of these three, do you think, was a neighbor to the man who fell into the hands of the robbers?' He said, 'The one who showed mercy'. Jesus said to him, 'Go and

The Golden Rule

do likewise'" Luke 10:25-37.

Religious leaders, power brokers and impostors were constantly trying to stop him with a barrage of tough questions. Jesus' style of handling such tough questions contrasts sharply with that of Saint Paul. The apostle Paul wrapped concepts in theological words and gave formal explanation. In careful prose, Paul patiently probed such complex concepts as forgiveness and justification. Jesus, speaking to restless crowds of thousands, communicated the same message in stories. Those stories express the message as well as any scholarly work.

2) **For people to understand what he said, they had to listen.** He urged them to do just that (Matt 15:10). Not content with such persuasion, he double-checked if they really understood his words, since he was addressing a cross-section drawn from different backgrounds (Matt 13:51). By following this method, Jesus employed one of the basics in communication: Understanding and being understood, through careful listening. If one did not understand, how would one respond? Conscious of the limitations of the listening crowds, Jesus avoided long arguments. Instead, emphasizing the need for people to change their behavior, he adapted his message to their level, never

overburdening them (John 16:12).

3) With Jesus it was not a monologue, a one-way street in the traffic of words. He liked **involving his listeners,** inviting them to participate, challenging them to put on their thinking caps. He quizzed them (Matt 18:12). And when they had donned their thinking caps, he astounded them with logical arguments and **earthy common sense.** The passage below illustrates the point: "No one sews a piece of un-shrunk cloth on an old cloak, for the patch pulls away from the cloak, and a worse tear is made. Neither is new wine put into old wineskins; otherwise, the skins burst, and the wine is spilled, and the skins are destroyed; but new wine is put into fresh wineskins, and so both are preserved" Matt 9:16-17. His listeners understood the situations and related to them readily.

4) What was his attitude to these listeners? He respected their freedom. Compassionately, he proposed, but **did not impose**. For example, a section of his disciples negatively responded to one of his teachings, and decided to no longer walk with him (John 6:60). Jesus did not call back these dissenters and dilute his teaching to win their loyalty. On another occasion, when a rich young man walked away from Jesus, unable to respond positively to the option Jesus offered him, of selling all

he had to follow him; he did not call him back to negotiate conditions for discipleship.

5) Since his listeners had studied scripture (the Old Testament), Jesus often quoted passages from it to connect with a point he was trying to make. When quoting from scripture, Jesus knew he was on common ground because many of his listeners had not just read scripture but memorized passages from it. He chose lines from scripture very appropriately. When the Pharisees accused the hungry apostles of plucking and eating grain on the Sabbath, Jesus quoted what King David had done in the past (Matt 12:3). By doing that, he was using the proven method of **reinforcing existing beliefs** of his listeners.

6) Jesus used clever **rejoinders and repartee** with telling effect. Those who dared to trap him had to be careful; very careful. Usually their tactics backfired as Jesus expertly redirected their questions on them. His debating skills were so sharp that his opponents were often impaled on them. Watch this: "He left that place and entered their synagogue; a man was there with a withered hand, and they asked him, 'Is it lawful to cure on the Sabbath?' so that they might accuse him. He said to them, 'Suppose one of you has only one sheep and it falls into a pit on

the Sabbath; will you not lay hold of it and lift it out? How much more valuable is a human being than a sheep! So it is lawful to do good on the Sabbath.'" Matt 12:9-12.

7) When some of the Pharisees and Sadducees tried to tease him with awkward questions, the technique of **Question for Question** worked effectively, as in the situation that follows: "Some Pharisees came, and to test him they asked, 'Is it lawful for a man to divorce his wife?' He answered them, 'What did Moses command you?'" Mark 10:2-3. When he had their answer to his question, he chose to answer. At other times, when he knew that the question was genuine, and not intended to test him, he chose to answer the question completely.

8) Whether he spoke with his disciples or the crowd, Jesus was the epitome of **courtesy** (Luke 7:40). And his idea of courtesy included slipping in a lesson on etiquette at table. "When he noticed how the guests chose the places of honor, he told them a parable. 'When you are invited by someone to a wedding banquet, do not sit down at the place of honor, in case someone more distinguished than you has been invited by your host; and the host who invited both of you may come and say to you, 'give this person your place', and then in disgrace you would start to

The Golden Rule

take the lowest place. But when you are invited, go and sit down at the lowest place, so that when your host comes, he may say to you, `Friend, move up higher'; then you will be honored in the presence of all who sit at table with you'". Luke 14:7-10. Discern his skill in communicating the lesson. He **stressed on the benefit**, the advantage, the honor the person would get by following his suggestion. To motivate someone to do something, show him how he will benefit. That is a tip that good communicators offer us. Jesus used the method with distinction.

9) His communication was always **relevant** – to his audience and to the occasion. In Luke 15 the Pharisees and Scribes complain that Jesus kept the company of sinners. He replies them by narrating three parables: The Lost Sheep (3-7), The Lost Coin (8-10) and The Lost Son, known as the Prodigal Son (11-32). Notice that he addresses the difficulty his listeners have in reconciling the presence of a holy person in the midst of wrong-doers. How can a Rabbi, like him, befriend sinners? Using the parables he explains why he is compassionate to sinners. He will not join them in wrong doing, but gently and patiently lead them from vice to virtue. The crowds listening to him are drawn from a mix of shepherds, flock-owners, fathers and mothers and all who have

Chapter 14 | The Communicator

a lasting interest in money. That is why they have no problem in relating to his message, as he uses their situations and their idiom – sheep, money and children. Eloquently, he blends the context with the message, to teach his lesson. The fit is perfect. Going after the lost is his purpose; redeeming the sinner is his priority. Reconciling the wrong-doer with God is a responsibility that no one can shirk, he concludes.

10) Look carefully at the audiences Jesus addresses. Is he talking to one person, his apostles, a crowd, or his opponents? He treats each differently. It seemed that he took words, scrubbed them clean, washed them in running water and laid them before his listeners. They sparkled. The sparkle came from the **figures of speech** he used with practiced ease. "I have said these things to you in figures of speech" John 16:25. There was liberal use of vivid similes in his speech. In Matt 10:16 we have an example: "See, I am sending you like sheep into the midst of wolves; so be wise as serpents and innocent as doves".

Original metaphors punctuated his speech. Describing his followers as the salt and light of the earth, Jesus said: "You are the salt of the earth; but if salt has lost its taste, how can its saltiness be restored? It is no longer good for anything, but is thrown out and trampled underfoot. You are the light of the world. A city built on a hill cannot be hid. No one after lighting a lamp puts it under the bushel basket, but on the lamp stand and it gives light to all in the house. In the same way, let your light shine before others" Matt 5:13-16. Metaphorically, he identified himself as the true vine (John 15:1), and the Good Shepherd (John 10:11). Speaking to his apostles, he compared their mission to fishing (Mathew 4:19) and harvesting (Mathew 9:37).

Occasionally, he used the hyperbole with stunning effect. The following verse is an example: "Again I tell you, it is easier for a camel to go through the eye of a needle than for someone who is rich to enter the kingdom of God" Matt 19:24. With the hyperbole, the statement is difficult to understand, to say the least. Minus the hyperbole, Jesus was suggesting that we should not get obsessed with, or attached to money. He selectively used the epigram: "The greatest among you will be your servant" Matt 23:11. And the Paradox had his listeners wondering: "For those who want to save their life will lose it, and those who lose their life for my sake will find it" Matt 16:25. He loved ironies and little riddles: "But many who are first will be last, and the last will be first" Matt 19:30. And in Matt 7: 9-10, he referred to a father who would not give his son a stone when the boy asked for bread, or give him a serpent when he wanted fish. His deft play of words was not lost on listeners when he said: "You blind guides! You strain out a gnat (Armaic - galma) but swallow a camel (Armaic-gamla)" Matt 23: 24. Sparing use of rhetoric gave his statements a rare verve: "Are grapes gathered from thorns, or figs from thistles?" Matt 7:16

11) How would one describe the **imagery** he brought to his speech? "Consider the lilies, how they grow: they neither toil nor spin; yet I tell you, even Solomon in all his glory was not clothed like one of these". Luke 12:27

12) Jesus spiced his talks with **axioms,** dictums and expressions that were seemingly trite, but couched profound meaning. "For where your treasure is, there your heart will be also" Luke 12:34. And, "Can a blind person guide a blind person?" Luke 6:39 and "One sows and another reaps" John 4:37. Pithy, power-packed punch lines (the alliteration is intended).

13) In the three years of his public ministry Jesus was constantly answering questions raised by friends and foes. In the process, **his list of questions** was not shortened: "But who do you

say I am?" Matt 16:15; and, "Do you want to be made well?" John 5:6.

14) Jesus was serious in his communication; never flippant. But there were times when his listeners could not help smiling when they caught the **funny tilt**. "Why do you see the speck in your neighbor's eye, but do not notice the log in your own eye? Or, how can you say to your neighbor, 'Let me take the speck out of your eye' while the log is in your own eye?" Matt 7:3-4

15) Sometimes, Jesus used the very situation, the **context** in which they were, to give his listeners a message: "He sat down opposite the treasury, and watched the crowd putting money into the treasury. Many rich people put in large sums. A poor widow came and put in two small copper coins, which are worth a penny. Then he called his disciples and said to them, 'Truly I tell you, this poor widow has put in more than all those who are contributing to the treasury, for all of them have contributed out of their abundance. But she out of her poverty has put in everything she had, all she had to live on'" Mark 12:41-44.

16) Jesus did not compromise his teaching. His listeners knew that he was **uniquely consistent** in his thought process.

Chapter 14 | The Communicator

Pope John Paul II was emphatic on how Jesus' words and deeds are 'never separable' from his life. His convictions were deep-rooted and strong. His words conveyed those convictions and his actions were consistent with his words. Everything tied up, without a contradiction. He was singularly unique.

Jesus had several titles given to him. But the most commonly used was teacher. In his role as teacher, his communication skills found full play. He was known to use the precise diction of a teacher, which combined remarkably with his limitless patience in reaching out to those he was teaching. Like his versatile personality, his communication had variety and class, simplicity and profound meaning, pin-pointed appeal and unrelenting persuasive power. Just like the drop that hollows the stone not by force, but by falling often, Jesus persuaded his listeners gently, but without giving up. As a good communicator, he knew his audience (drawn from different castes, classes, regions, professions, political systems), and adapted to their needs. And they responded.

What were those words that described his impact on them? Amazed, Astonished, Astounded, Spellbound.

The Golden Rule

Chapter 15

Leadership and Change

"Change is not merely necessary to life. It is life."

~ Alvin Tofler.

Only leaders who walk tall can initiate and empower change. Those who cannot walk tall, trip on their own feet and fall; many do. Leaders who are dwarfed by the compromises they make cannot fill the huge footprints of leaders who walk tall. They step into one print but cannot reach the next. For them the struggle is unending.

In simple terms, management is coping with complexity, and leadership is initiating and coping with change. A professional should manage both. When he effectively manages his resources he is handling complex situations. Built into those complex situations are changes he must usher in speedily and decisively, despite popular vote against them. At times he is alone, trusting that the change he is trying to bring about will prompt his

The Golden Rule

teammates to support him, later. Sometimes, even that solace is not his. Yet he must move on, to put into action what he believes he should. Peter Drucker, the peerless management guru, believed that leadership and management are inseparable; they fuse for producing results. That is why his concept of management was known as the practical way to quantifiable outcomes.

Complete agreement does not exist as to what exactly constitutes the job of a professional. Different researchers and writers have tried to examine his functions and put down their thoughts. But a satisfactory homogenous description is difficult to find. One thing is clear though, the professional must cope with complexities that proceed from the very act of effectively managing resources. Some writers give importance to the profit maximization objective. They say that he must strive for profits, at all costs. He owes it to the stakeholders. Others think differently. They believe there is more to it than just money. They believe that a value-driven manager can set the tone for a value-system, in the organization. And profits will follow. Almost like suggesting to a marketing manager to focus on customer satisfaction and customer delight. Once he does that he need have no worry because profits will follow.

Chapter 15 | Leadership and Change

A report appeared in The Economist of April 24, 2010, that Paul Polman, boss of Unilever, told the Financial Times: "I do not work for the Shareholder, to be honest; I work for the consumer, the customer---. I am not driven and I do not drive this business model by driving Shareholder value". Maximizing customer satisfaction or Customer-driven Capitalism are terms that are increasingly endorsed by CEOs.

Jim Tregbig, of Tandom, said that every person is a human being and deserves to be treated as one. The late J.R.D. Tata had similar points to make. Kenneth Blanchard emphatically writes: "There is nothing so unequal, as the equal treatment of unequals". Cooper Procter of Procter and Gamble ran the company with the slogan: "Do what is right". Theodore Vail of AT & T stressed superior customer service. Robert Townsend wrote: "If you have a policy manual, publish the Ten Commandments". The organization culture put together by such professionals will determine objectives - which are chased in different ways. Each organization sets in motion a flow of activity that is distinct, and hopefully right for the situation. What emerges is that the leadership style at the top decides how the organization is managed. The direction he gives the organization sets it on a path.

The Golden Rule

And it travels at a pace he chooses to give it.

In this mold the leader is a change agent; changing vision, changing methods, changing the bottom line.

To make changes he must have a clear vision. What is vision? It is the big picture, larger than life, that he is drawn to, and tries to actualize; a magnificent obsession. Vision is the engine that drives leadership. It helps the leader anticipate and plan, with a consuming passion. Vision means foresight and direction; getting others to share the vision and motivating them to pursue it. Without vision the leader is dead. The Institution is dead.

To actualize his vision, the leader must take decisions. And decision making becomes an important activity, as Lou Prichett stresses in Stop Paddling and start rocking the boat: "One trait of the true leader is decisiveness; if you can't make a decision you probably aren't cut out to be a leader". In the process, a leader can come face to face with paradoxes, which he must resolve, through enlightened decision making. Jack Welch has a point to make: "Effective leadership involves the acceptance and management of paradox". In effect he is making two points. First, accept the paradoxical situation. Do not resent it. You have to live

Chapter 15 | Leadership and Change

with it. Second, plan the management of the situation.

It follows that the leader must see every problem, even a paradox, as an opportunity which will take him closer to actualizing his vision. Alan Stoneman, former President of Purex Corporation said: "We have no problems here; all are opportunities". Mother Teresa had something similar to say. She said that a difficulty or a problem was not a cross but a blessing. Put differently, she was trying to tell us that the way we see the problem, is the problem. Almost identical thoughts were paraphrased by Stephen R Covey when he explained that effective people are not problem-oriented. They are opportunity-oriented. They feed the opportunity and starve the problem.

In his problem solving, or opportunity-feeding attempts, the leader must build trust. His team must trust him. So must others, who transact with him. Otherwise his attempts to problem-solve will fail.

Shiv Khera lists some qualities that help build trust:

- Respect for others
- Fairness

The Golden Rule

- Openness
- Congruence
- Integrity and honesty
- Character

Without respect for others, leadership fails. It is the corner stone in building relationships. This quality possibly comes from a win-win attitude; the abundance mentality. There is plenty out there for everybody. So why trample on another to get to where you want to go? Perhaps he will help you get there faster if only he sees that you respect him and his perceptions.

From respect for people, is born fairness. You would not want to win by making him lose. Instead, can he also win, even as you try to win? The fair leader is respected, is admired and is idolized because deep down all of us want to be fair, but only a few of us get to being that. There are very few who can objectively and fair-mindedly take decisions; no matter what the consequences.

Coupled with fairness is openness. He has nothing to hide. He is unafraid. Henry Ford II included openness in his list of qualities for a professional. When the leader has respect for others, a sense of fair play and openness in concluding transactions, there is synergy in what he does. Then double standards have no space in his mental make-up. His words and actions show a unique oneness. There is congruence.

In such a leader, one expects honesty and integrity; the key ingredients to truth. Such a leader is held in high esteem. He is morally sound and worthy of trust. Donald M. Kendall, one-time Chairperson of Pepsico had integrity right on top of his list of professional attributes. Noah Dietrich (who managed the Howard Hughes Empire for 32 years) identified honesty and candor as top qualities for professionals.

Finally, when you find character in him, the puzzle is solved. He deserves to be the leader. Character is an intangible which is difficult to define, since it is strikingly individualistic. But character, when absent, negates the role. He is no longer fit to be the leader.

Successful leaders are known to have traits that have been identified by Henry Mintzberg. These traits are: brevity, variety, action-orientation and strong oral communication. Such traits lend them some dynamism. You spot them readily. They are the Achievers. These Achievers are flexible. Not bound by tradition. Not shackled by obdurate mindsets. Paul H. Dainty and Moreen Anderson, point out that such leaders are positive. They are given to situational leadership. They are not despondent or negative; conservative or overly cautious. Kenneth Blanchard, Patricia Zigarmi and Drea Zigarmi, writing in Leadership and the One Minute Manager, describe the style of the situational leader. He uses different strokes for different folk. He directs when necessary. That is when he gives specific instructions and closely supervises the task. He switches to coaching, when that style is appropriate. In the coaching style the leader directs, explains and invites suggestions from the one he is coaching. And he changes to the supporting style when that can make a difference. In the supporting style he shares the decision making responsibility with his team fellow. And he delegates, when his team mate is ready. When he delegates, he hands over decision making and problem solving responsibility to his team fellow.

Such flexibility makes him accessible to his team mates. They come to him because they know that they will be treated with understanding. They are not afraid of a rebuff. In time they want to be part of the leader's vision; which culminates in shared values. The team begins to see the leader's vision and is prepared to work for that vision with commitment.

In such a framework, how does Jesus fit? Take his vision. In the three years of his public ministry, Jesus did not dither. His goal was set and he pursued it unfailingly. He communicated that vision to his team and motivated them enough to make his vision their own. In later years the apostles lived and died in defense of his vision, which had become theirs.

In arriving at decisions, he was decisive; not vacillating; not wavering. Whether he was selecting a team or empowering them or challenging the system or confronting the hypocrites or choosing locations to visit (to spread his messages), or synagogues to go in and teach, he did not hesitate; even if the decision was tough; even when a paradox had to be resolved.

Look at the number of times he converted a problem into a teaching-opportunity. The adulteress is brought to him, so that he may condemn her. Her accusers think he has no way out. Yet she is acquitted, not just because he forgives her, but because he turns the law back on them. His listeners learn that every law

The Golden Rule

should be fully comprehended before it is administered. Should tax be paid to Caesar, they ask. A 'yes' would mean that the rebels who wanted freedom from Rome would see him as a stooge of Rome. A 'no' would mean going against Caesar. Give to Caesar what belongs to Caesar and to God what belongs to Him, he avers. He used each situation not just to silence his opponents, but chiefly to teach all his listeners a lesson. And, he used his power without being oppressive.

We find many occasions in the Gospels when people place their faith in him – they trusted him. His apostles trusted him because he was open and fair and honest; because there was no dichotomy between his words and deeds (he preached forgiveness and readily forgave even his sworn enemies); because he genuinely respected and loved people and was compassionate; and because of his exemplary conduct and his faultless character. He showed that a true leader needed no props, no crutches. His personality, not given to judging others, attracted both the ordinary folk and the open minded upper classes.

His teachings and debates were short, to the point and directed at action. His skill in verbal communication was so outstanding that Thomas Jefferson referred to it as 'the sublimest

Chapter 15 | Leadership and Change

eloquence'. People wondered at the ease with which he debated with the doctors of law and demolished their arguments.

He was an action-oriented leader; not laid back or given to passive responses. For him each moment was important. Each day was one day less in his 3-year ministry. Much was to be done and he could not wait or relax. And of his situational management skills, we have plenty of proof in the Gospels. Carefully examine the different methods he uses to tutor Peter. Watch the different styles he uses to contend with the opposition. He was constantly adapting to the situation. He did not get stale or predictable, because he was continually finding new ways of doing things; coming up with situation-specific solutions.

Employing such a formidable combination of qualities he brought about changes that were far-reaching. He toppled established practices, including the strict observances of the Sabbath. Totally unafraid, he challenged the archaic system, proposing a non-violent method of resolving disputes, strongly recommending forgiveness instead of retaliation, and daring his listeners to try out a new way of life – love of God and love of neighbors. Through the turmoil, he himself stood out as an example of unconditional love. He was uniquely consistent.

The Golden Rule

What do we notice when a strong wind has passed? A lot of things are out of place. So was society, when Jesus passed that way. Beliefs were questioned. Many practices seemed meaningless. A new order was in the making because a new kind of professional was at work.

Chapter 16
The Combination is Synergetic

"A good head and a good heart are always a formidable combination."

Nelson Mandela.

After a disturbing session on Friday, the group was more relaxed and expectant today. A day in between had given them time to think. Reading the material they were given, they were better equipped to ask questions and provide answers. They also knew what was coming. It was 4:05 pm on Saturday, as they reassembled to attend to unfinished business.

Deepak Chopra rose and spoke with his customary courtesy: "Gentlemen and Ms. Desai thank you for coming on a Saturday evening; and coming on time. I take it that you have read the material you collected yesterday and feel richer by the experience."

Latif Basha, who had raised objections on Friday, seemed

The Golden Rule

anxious to speak: "Mr. Chopra, besides reading the extra material you gave me, I found the time to read Mathew."

"You have given today's meeting a good start," Deepak commended him.

"In the additional material you gave us, the passages from the Bible stand out; there is only sparse commentary. The passages speak for themselves," Lokesh inferred.

"Like pearls strung together, they glitter." Sunil's simile gave Lokesh's comment some brilliance.

"Lokesh and Sunil, thank you for your helpful deductions." Deepak, who was conscious that much had to be done and only two hours to do them, was quick to respond, and continued: "Yesterday, we discussed the 360° appraisal. We also discussed the attitudes, skills, habits and knowledge attributes of a super model. And we set you thinking on Jesus. For a while, let us look at the four factors and apply them to Jesus. What can we put down as the attitudes, skills, habits, and knowledge of Jesus?"

"He was honest and fair," Latif declared.

"He was positive and open," Mahesh added.

Chapter 16 | The Combination is Synergetic

"He was courageous and outspoken," Deb stated.

"May I put down those points under the head of attitudes?" Deepak asked.

"Yes," Sunil agreed.

Deepak then wrote down the points on the white board and turning to his audience, asked: "What more?"

"Towards wealth and money, he had a detached attitude," Kiran added.

"I think he was a people-person. Like a magnet attracting iron filings, he attracted people," Muthukrishnan was effusive.

"I think he was consistent in what he said and did. There was no double-speak," Kiran made another point.

"He comes across as a very committed person. He had a mission and he was wedded to that mission," Satish said very purposefully and added: "A self effacing incident comes to mind. Jesus has been with the crowds for the whole day working wondrous deeds for them. An eventful day comes to a close. Early the next day he goes out. The apostles look for him. After much searching they find him and tell him of the huge impact he has had on the people. Even now, they say, people are looking for him everywhere. Instead of going to them to be congratulated and praised, he tells his apostles that they will leave immediately for other places where they will have to spread the Good News. Unlike most of us, who would go after applause and distraction, he stayed focused on his mission".

"Thank you. Satish that was an important point you made. We have put down these points, under his attitude. Let us now move to his skills." Deepak was polite, yet firm.

"He was a great communicator; an excellent debater. I do not know of anyone who can match his communication skills." Deb offered his opinion.

"His skill in resolving conflicts, in handling difficult situations deftly, is something we can all learn from." Lokesh spoke up.

"His situational management skill was extraordinary; with individuals, or his apostles, or the crowd, or his tormentors. Remarkable!" Sunil observed.

"What a story teller he was! So creative; so beautifully crafted were his stories," Rahul remarked.

Chapter 16 | The Combination is Synergetic

"Shall we now take up his habits? The idea is to get to the essentials; the important points. We are not planning to make an exhaustive list," Deepak explained.

"Jesus was the hands-on type; up front, saying things, doing things and giving the lead." Lokesh's opinion was well received.

"He was very hard working; always on the move. But he carefully planned breaks for his apostles from the punishing schedule he followed. That was thoughtful of him." Deb certainly enjoyed the occasional breaks he took.

"Self-disciplined and time conscious, he did not indulge in wasteful effort," Latif was speaking again.

"Jesus was earnest about setting the right example. Besides the unmatched example he set from the cross, he gave us an enduring example when he washed the feet of his apostles. I cannot visualize any CEO doing that." Satish showed that he had reflected on the Gospels.

"Satish, you are right. Jesus inspires through the examples he sets in many ways. I only hope we can follow some of his sterling qualities. Now, shall we move on to his knowledge?"

The Golden Rule

Deepak asked.

"The Gospels do not say how he acquired so much knowledge. But he knew the scriptures well enough to challenge the doctors of law. He could relate to business, legal matters, customs, nature and so many more subjects. At that time he could have been called a walking encyclopedia. Remember, the people were spellbound when he spoke." Rahul had read all the four Gospels more than once, but he made no mention of it.

"Let us try and wrap up this part of our discussion, shall we? We have all the points you listed. The list is impressive. My question to you is: Do you find something wanting? Could Jesus have done something, he did not do? Was there any gap, which he should have bridged?" Deepak worded his question cautiously.

"Yes, I think he should have spoken up during his trial and crucifixion. He let them take advantage of him. He could have silenced them, as he silenced others in the past. Even Pilate was just waiting for some signal from him to set him free. But he was silent." Latif spoke with anguish.

"And I think he should have got one of his apostles to document all that he said and did. We have the Gospels. But

Chapter 16 | The Combination is Synergetic

chances are that we have missed a lot because it was not written at the time of the event." Satish spoke as though it was a personal loss.

"Let us take your two points. First, you say he should have spoken up at his trial. Think of it. His adversaries were fixated on crucifying him. They were in no mood to listen to him. Jesus knew that it would serve no purpose if he tried to explain matters. So he chose not to speak. In fact, his silence amazed them. And they wondered at the strength of his character. Second, you say that he should have got someone to record all that he said and did. He could have. But notice that he was not particular in recording his actions. He even discouraged people from speaking of the miracles he performed. What he wanted was that people reflect on what he said and try to change. Come to think of it, even if he wanted them to record his words and deeds, who among his apostles was equipped to do that; perhaps Mathew? And Mathew did give us a fairly exhaustive account. John's Gospel was born of great reflection. That could not have been written without reflection. It had to wait. John states at the end of his Gospel that there was much more to be recorded. Why he, who was with Jesus through the three years, did not write more will remain unanswered. Mark and Luke were not among his apostles. So, recording events into a diary when Jesus was with them did not fit into the scheme of things." The homework that Deepak had done was evident. "Anything else?" he checked.

"Not that we can think of for now. He is a towering personality. We are not equal to the task of picking holes in his life and works." Rahul confessed.

"Well then, that puts things in place. What comes across from the points you made are that Jesus was a man ahead of his times, committed to a lofty Mission. He was prepared to work very hard to make it happen. He was not just competent, but wise; and wisdom we know comes from contemplation and positive action. He was a people-person, ready to help anyone in need. He brought about changes through his teachings, powerfully communicated, and through conduct that was exemplary. He was genuine. Never fake. Would that make sense?" Agreement with Deepak was unanimous.

"Mr. Alex Thomas, your turn". Deepak said this as he went back to his seat. Alex stood up. He looked impressive in his steel-gray Armani suit. The button-down Louis Philippe white shirt

Chapter 16 | The Combination is Synergetic

was without blemish. The maroon Van Heusen tie with black spots stood out against his dark jacket. The cuff links he wore glinted in the bright conference room. All eyes were riveted on him.

"You are marketing professionals who should understand the connection that I shall try to establish. Someone wisely said: 'Enter through their door to exit through yours'. I am trying to explain it in your idiom so that you get the message. Jesus was a marketing man; a customer-oriented Professional. Let us see how. Take the variables in marketing. You have a company, marketing products to customers, in conditions that could be favorable or unfavorable and having to contend with competition that could be fierce. What have I said? I said that there are 4 variables involved - the company, the customer, conditions and competition – 4Cs of marketing. Now take the marketing mix. You have a product, sold at a price, through a distribution network, we call place, with the help of the right promotion. That means we have 4 more variables: Product, Price, Place and Promotion – the 4Ps of marketing. In all there are 8 variables. I said that Jesus was a marketing man. Let us see how he managed these variables. What was his company? Call it, if you like, Jesus Christ Inc.; small; no equity; yet full of enthusiasm and zeal; mission-propelled. In three

The Golden Rule

years they were operating in different parts of Palestine. No corporate office. No stationery. Perhaps that was the first paperless office. No computers. No cell phones. No banks to fund projects. They had ambitious plans of going international; but were down to earth in handling day-to-day situations. No targets or budgets; only strategies for market situations.

Who were his customers? Farmers and fisherman, the sick and infirm, the poor and the rich, the famous and the notorious made up the wide spectrum of customers he served. No one was excluded. A large mass market, if you get what I mean. Did he segment his market? In a way he did. He responded readily to the needy. That segment seemed to be his target group. But he was prepared to transact with all: The Roman Centurion, Nicodemus (the influential Pharisee) and Zacchaeus, the Chief Tax Collector; just anybody.

What were the conditions in which he operated? The Jews were a subjugated lot. Rome ruled with an iron hand. The Jews were therefore an oppressed people, who had to find hope in something; that hope was the liberator, the savior, who was to come and free them from the oppressor, sword wielding and lance-thrusting; the fighting hero. The Messiah who appeared,

Chapter 16 | The Combination is Synergetic

Jesus, was the anti-climax. They felt let down. A good bit of their resentment toward him was born of their disappointment. So, they were suspicious of what he said and did. Their response was tardy. Not from the ordinary people; but from the upper classes. The conditions, to say the least, were not favorable. Jesus probably made things worse for himself by exposing the hypocrisy of the opposition. And they were bent on stopping his advancement. The competition was really fierce. In such circumstances, what did Jesus have to offer? What was his product? He offered his customers a concept. He was into concept marketing where there was nothing to touch, feel or smell; only an idea; a very different idea. Different from the one the Jews had been taught; beyond the law they knew. The very newness was startling. What really was the product? Love - love god, love yourself and love your neighbor. The product was so advanced that people could not comprehend it; the dimensions were difficult to measure. When 'an eye for an eye' was the way of life, how could love and forgiveness fit? When intrigue, hate and vengeance were commonly traded in, how could his product be bartered? Yet, Jesus was all set to give his product an edge through personal example. He would not rest till the market gave his product a fair chance.

What was the price he expected for his product? No money. No goods in exchange. No deferred payment. No credit card payment. What he asked for was only faith. Would they want to believe in him? Would they choose to trust him? That was all he wanted.

Did he incur marketing costs? Very little cost, because they traveled on foot and sometimes in a boat. He threw no parties to entertain clients. His hospitality was the sharing of his meager rations. He sent no greeting cards at festival time and had no communication costs. His small needs were met by people who began to share his beliefs; a fraternity that was growing by the day.

What did he do about place; a distribution network? He had no distributors and retailers. Instead he and his team decided to deliver the product directly to his customers. Jesus led from up-front, meeting his customers and delivering the product to them, literally on a one-to-one basis. Although he addressed groups, he was concerned about each person in the group. He spotted their needs and transacted with them not for a single sale,

Chapter 16 | The Combination is Synergetic

but for building a relationship. He knew that if trust was built, relationships would peak and transactions would repeat. He was into relationship marketing. He had no insurance cover and no claims to be settled. No transit-time restrictions. The delivery system he devised was so successful that his customers came to him in droves to do repeat business with him. As he expanded his team from 12 to 82, the new team fellows joined in the supply chain management, though logistics management was centrally monitored. Some of his customers accepted his product with less understanding. But most with nothing short of awe.

What about promotion? Advertising, the way we know it now, was not in vogue. He communicated his message directly and in simple terms. He got to the head and heart of his listener and to the heart of the subject. What techniques did he use? He used parables or stories and examples drawn from family and work life. He spoke their lingo, their idiom. Most understood. And how did the message spread? Not through billboards, posters or hand bills. The message spread only through word-of- mouth testimony. Those who came to hear him told others. More came. They too heard him and told still more. The numbers swelled. Testimony, as we know is a powerful medium, and promotion, not in our mundane sense, was at work.

How did he position himself? He occupied a position that was easily identified because it was different. He took a position that opposed popular perception. The law promoted retaliation. Jesus said forgive your enemies; love those who offend you. He swung the pendulum to the other extreme. His customers could not but notice, and they were astounded.

And what happened to the additional 4 Ps? What we refer to as: People, Pace, Processes and Packaging. There is universal admission that Jesus was a people person; all the time building new bonds, mending broken bonds and concretizing relationships. His pace was hectic; constantly on the move. Alert to any situation he was half a step ahead of the opposition. He started when he was 30. When we look back at what he accomplished in three years, we are amazed. At 33 he was dead.

What were the processes involved? Whether delegating or instructing, healing the sick or feeding the poor, planning a trip to a distant location or visiting a synagogue for a discourse, all processes were simple, linked, and effective. There was no waste of time. No duplication of effort. No waste of any resource.

Chapter 16 | The Combination is Synergetic

How did he package his product? Not in polyethylene or cans, but in easily understood words. In stories that have been retold several thousand times down the centuries. In vivid examples. He packaged the product keeping his customer in mind. The way the customer would understand and accept the product.

Through 2000 years, more and more people are beginning to make sense of the very simple concept (product) that he promoted, because he combined head and heart in appealing to them. He used reason and emotion to touch their heads and hearts. As we do in marketing, Jesus looked at the situation from the customer's point of view.

So, you see Gentlemen and Kiran, Jesus was a marketing man, well into concept marketing, into relationship marketing. He was a specialist in CRM (customer relationship marketing). He tried to go beyond customer satisfaction to achieve customer delight. And he achieved it with distinction. I have seen it. You too will see it now." He paused, looked at his audience once more and said, "I thank you for your time and attention," and sat down. Not a word was spoken. Perhaps some wanted to applaud. But none did.

The Golden Rule

It was now Victor's turn. He looked animated and ready to go, but suggested a five minute break, when he found the smokers in the room fidgety.

Chapter 17

Empowering Professional Relationships

"It is more important to do the right thing, than to do things right."

~ Peter Drucker

As they reassembled, Victor lost no time in getting started.

"Gentlemen and Ms. Desai, to points made by Mr. Chopra and Mr. Thomas, let me add a few.

Jesus sought the transformation of human relations; which in simple terms, means motivating the individual to perform by recognizing his efforts, encouraging his performance and rewarding him suitably. Combining the human resources (which Mr Deepak Chopra represents) and human relations approaches, he spoke of the kingdom of God, not as something distant and unattainable, but as a very real brotherhood of mankind, where people could live in peace, with steadfast faith, joyous hope, and untiring love. He believed each person was capable of much. Each

The Golden Rule

had a potential to be realized. Spot that talent; develop it; allow it blossom, was how he saw it. The transformation of Mathew from tax collector to a loyal apostle is a case in point. The words of Scott Peck come to mind: 'All human interactions are opportunities either to learn or to teach'. Jesus taught and Mathew learned. Jesus spoke to the crowds and they listened – which was a step in the learning process. I have a slide here, which illustrates a very important point."

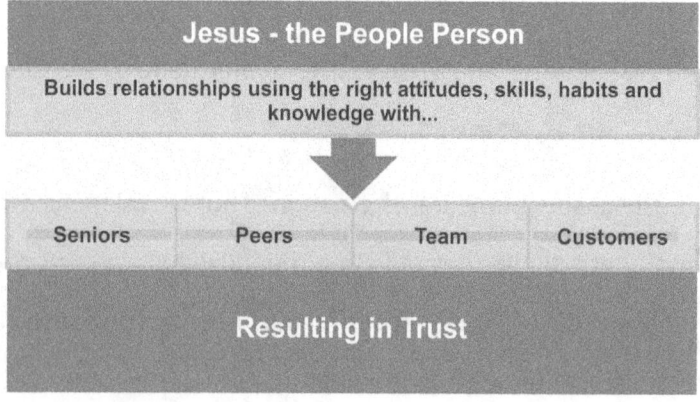

After the group had made notes from the slide, Victor continued: "Trust in a person is the highest tribute you can pay him. When people believed in him, when his apostles trusted him, Jesus received a compliment that we professionals crave for. Few

Chapter 17 | Empowering Professional Relationships

of us gain it in a professional-lifetime. Many of us retire before tasting of its sweetness.

Yesterday, Mr. Chopra, spoke to you on the 360° appraisal. He said that it was an effective tool to measure the kind of relationships we build with different segments of people. After spending many hours discussing the new system, the Vice Presidents and I attempted a 360° appraisal of Jesus. Mr. Chopra has worked on our comments and prepared a summary that highlights a few essential points. No appraisal for a person like Jesus can be complete." So saying, Victor put up the summary. With the slide up, he paused for a long time. They had taken notes, but kept looking at the slide, wanting to know more. Victor began slowly.

"Gentlemen and Ms. Desai this is an intriguing part of my presentation. By now you are familiar with the four quadrants in the 360 degree appraisal. The illustration in this slide is less important. It is just a rough representation of the four segments. The points in it are significant. May I have your undivided attention, as I take you through the points in the four quadrants? We had to work with a limitation. We could not interact directly with the different sources for the appraisal: seniors, peers,

The Golden Rule

teammates and customers. We could not administer questionnaires to them. Instead we had to depend on what we found in the Gospels; and make inferences. From the pages of history, those people spoke to us and helped us form opinions.

In the first 90° quadrant, reference is made only to seniors; how seniors viewed Jesus. In the second 180° quadrant, only responses from Peers, the new variable, find place. In fact it should hold information on both seniors and peers. To avoid repetition and clutter, we have focused on peers. Likewise, in the third 270° quadrant, relationship with the Team is appraised; subordinates, if you please. We have not repeated information from the first and second quadrants. And finally in the fourth 360° quadrant, we focus on the Customers. In effect the 360° appraisal is the sum total of what appears in the four quadrants. Is that clear?" It was clear to them.

"In each quadrant we record our overall assessment of Jesus for the corresponding variable. We have *Good* for the first, *Very Good* for the next and *Excellent* for the third and fourth. Then we explain why we gave Jesus those overall assessments. Yesterday, Mr. Chopra gave you a fairly long list of Jesus' attributes as a people-person, team-person and so on. In the summary you are reading now, we have not reproduced all those points. We have picked a few.

In the first quadrant, we have given Pilate the status of a superior; not his immediate superior, but as the Roman Governor, he exercised rights over people in that region. Jesus belonged to that region; therefore the connection. Pilate respected Jesus and was amazed at his regal ways; and tried three times to release him. In fact he found no fault in him, but decreed the crucifixion more out of fear of Rome. Anyone setting himself up as king challenged Caesar's throne. Jesus did not, but the high priests portrayed him as a usurper. The high priests were not Jesus' superiors. But in the structure of that time a Rabbi, was at least a level lower than the high priests. And Jesus was a Rabbi. That explains our giving some weight to their opinion of Jesus. We all know that their opinions were prejudiced. They feared his growing influence and the prospect of being side-lined and manipulated the crowds to scream for Jesus' death. To contain the threat that Jesus supposedly posed, they engineered his downfall by getting him crucified. Despite their villainous ways, they unwittingly and grudgingly paid him a compliment when they keenly and closely followed his actions and words; and the impact they had on people. The overall weight we have given the first quadrant is: Good. We must remember that, in the conventional sense, Jesus did not have a superior. Therefore, the rating given to him in the first quadrant need not carry much weight. The ratings in the other three quadrants are more important. Mr Chopra, when he has finished his investigations will teach us how to do a proper grading. Until then we shall settle for what we have now done.

The feedback from Peers appears in the second quadrant. If one were to look at Nicodemus, Zacchaeus, and some others as his peers, it is obvious that they occupied fairly high positions and were definitely socially and professionally above the apostles. These peers of Jesus listened to him, were edified by his example and followed his advice. Nicodemus even stood up for Jesus against the Council, jeopardizing his position among the Council members. Zacchaeus showed how seriously he took Jesus' example, when he chose to give up his money-grabbing ways. Our overall assessment is: Very Good. We have dropped a point or two here, because some of these peers were afraid to own up peerage or any association with Jesus, in the presence of the power-brokers. They preferred to seek his counsel late into the night to escape prying eyes.

Chapter 17 | Empowering Professional Relationships

The third quadrant is about the team. How did they respond to him? What had they to say? The reading material we gave you has many points on his relationship with the apostles. He gave them a Mission, and with them, pursued it relentlessly. He trained them and delegated powers to them. Loved them and protected them. Without reserve they obeyed him, and importantly, trusted him, giving up all that they called their own. What more can one expect? The assessment is: Excellent.

In the fourth quadrant we have feedback from his customers. What was his message to them? Love. Right through the three years of his public ministry he found different ways of putting this message across to them. He praised them and motivated them. He helped them and empathized with them. By example he showed that all his teachings can be practiced. Almost in return for all that he did for them, they followed him in increasing numbers. And many believed in him. Our overall assessment is: Excellent.

Now, you know that if more factors were put into it, we would have a more detailed illustration and a distinctly better rating. But we did a sample. Our sample speaks volumes to us.

The Golden Rule

In this appraisal, we cannot ignore the cowardly behavior of the apostles at the time of Jesus' arrest and crucifixion. We should try to understand why they behaved in the way they did. Their devotion to him was never in doubt, but fear of arrest, torture and death, made them flee. Like normal humans who put distance between themselves and danger, the apostles took flight. We also witness the rabid behavior of his customers, the common people, during the crucifixion. How do we explain that? Two points strike me. One, the common folk obeyed their priests and elders; such obedience was built into their psyche. These priests and elders, who had turned against Jesus because of jealousy, were inciting the people to demand his death; and the people followed the edicts of the priests. Two, mob-behavior is seldom rational. Trigger one section with a slogan and the others follow. Their turn-coat behavior at that time does not erase from memory the adulation and accolades they gave Jesus when he walked with them.

Jesus was a religious leader; we have no doubts. We have not gone into his religious teachings, except to center on a teaching that concerns us all: That no man is an island. He needs people around him. It is therefore appropriate that he learns to

Chapter 17 | Empowering Professional Relationships

live with them in a spirit of co-operation and co-existence; in a spirit of forgiveness; in perceiving the weaknesses of others with compassion, not accusation; and in building bridges, not barriers. Notice the way he reaches out to the thief on his right. Jesus has been tortured and tormented for several hours. He has not eaten. He has not slept. Every part of his body is in pain. Bleeding from wounds, his life is on the ebb. His friends have run away. The crowd mocks him to come down from the cross if he really is the miracle worker, they had seen on their streets. Pain and sorrow are his only companions. He feels abandoned by all. At this time the thief on his right asks Jesus to remember him. Jesus forgets his own pain and looks at another in pain. He does not accuse the thief. Instead, his heart goes out to him in friendship." Victor trailed off. He waited until he regained his voice. And then asked in an emotion-charged voice: "Could there be a truer example of reaching out to others?"

He paused again, and continued after a while. "We have tried to look at how he did what he did. What was his style? What were his skills? How did his attitude affect his relationships? Were his habits different from those of other successful professionals? We have tried to appraise him. And a picture of Jesus is forming

The Golden Rule

that we cannot but admire; of a Master Model who forges and strengthens relationships. We have, no doubt, much to learn from him. His greatness and strength are like the ocean. We can dip our little buckets and draw out of it. Those buckets will suffice, as long as we do not stop drawing from the source.

What was Jesus' formula to successful relationships? I asked myself that question many times; and came up with a rather short answer: **The Golden Rule.** Do to others what you would want them do to you. The Rule is born of intrinsic discipline. Quoting Scott Peck again, I shall reinforce that point: 'Without discipline we can solve nothing'. We want people to respect us; to listen to us; to give us affection; to trust us; not to hurt us. If only we remember that others would want the same treatment from us, our double standards would vanish. Our relationships would thrive. We would excel in building good relationships because of the discipline we exercise. Jesus showed that no foe could gain advantage over him because of the discipline he had in blunting hate with love. Hate lost its knife-edge. In doing that, he was proactive, always taking the first step towards friendship. The apostles gained strength in the warmth of his personality. His customers found him disarmingly acceptable. That is why people said that he did everything well. And they were spellbound.

Put differently, we build strong relationships by living the Golden Rule, which is obeying Jesus' command to love others as we love ourselves. Undoubtedly, it is a tall order; an extremely difficult project; effort that could repeatedly end in lack of success (not failure; failure is a strong negative word. I would rather not use it). Yet, it makes sense to cherish the Golden Rule as a lofty goal and pursue it. Why? As humans we believe that we are masters of the world. As professionals we imagine that we can conquer odds against us. No wonder we try to attain the unattainable. We climb our mountains; we run our sprints in record-breaking time; we sail uncharted waters; we chase huge targets. The quest for new frontiers never stops. Wasn't it Robert Browning who asked: 'Ah, but a man's reach should exceed his grasp, or what's a heaven for?'

There is another reason why the Golden Rule makes sense. Dale Carnegie, in his very popular book, How to win friends and influence people, states a few relevant facts. He writes that, in different words, Zoraster taught the Rule to his followers in Persia, 2500 years ago. At about the same time, Buddha, in India, taught his disciples to value others as they value themselves. Confucius

The Golden Rule

and Lao-Tse, in China, propagated the same idea. The Jews in their holy book support the same value. And, Hindus in their sacred scriptures uphold the same belief. Dale Carnegie is trying to tell us that Jesus is not alone in proposing the Golden Rule; others too share the same belief. The Rule is universal. It cuts across cultures and travels across borders to appeal to all of humankind. And we are part of that humankind. That should make the Golden Rule our objective, difficult though it seems.

Of particular interest to us, at this stage, should be Jesus' injunction to pursue excellence and his Situational Management style. Remember how he exhorted his Apostles: 'Be Perfect'. His dictum to us is to strive for perfection. In our attempts we may not succeed; but we ought to get up quickly and try again. Take us. Don't we let frustration get the better of us? How often we give up? How often we settle for second best? How often we take up a task ill-prepared? Certainly, we should seriously take Jesus' call for perfection. Only then will our teammates and others, who transact with us, spot in us something that they admire, and want to emulate.

Situational Management stems from the vital fact that each of us is different, unique; and therefore to be dealt with

Chapter 17 | Empowering Professional Relationships

carefully and differently. Whether we direct, coach, support or delegate, we need to understand the person we are transacting with and adapt to the situation, using our best to bring out the best in him or her. When we do that, our customers, vendors, other agencies (on the outside) and our teammates (on the inside) will see a new style in the way we transact; a personalized and purpose-driven style which will foster warm relationships and bring us results.

Reflecting on Situational Management, we must pause at our understanding of delegation. We want our seniors to delegate to us unconditionally, which is not wrong. But what do we do when we have to delegate to those who report to us? Are we ready to let go? More often than not we make a mockery of the idea, only to be mocked at by those who suffer at our hands. Some alarm bells are ringing. Are we listening?"

Alex answered the rhetorical question: "Be sure. We are listening to you and your message."

Victor: "Thank you Alex. I am sure you are speaking for the team." And continued: "Let us get down to practical dimensions. Not all customers give us pleasure in our transactions with them.

The Golden Rule

Some, internal and external, are difficult; bent on making life hard for us. To transact with them we have two options: be equally difficult or, be understanding. Being equally difficult is easy. Tit-for-tat is soaked in pleasure. We sense the thrill of exercising power over somebody. The very idea is pleasing. Yet, what is the result? Strained relationships and negative outcomes continue to challenge us. The irony in this option surfaces when that 'somebody' is more powerful than we are. With those who are weak we retaliate because we are not afraid of the consequences; but with powerful people we tend to be cautious. For example, can I hit out at my boss? Can I offend a big and powerful customer who contributes hugely to my revenue? Can I abuse a Government Officer who refuses to see things the way I see them? No, those actions would not be prudent. So, I am forced to exercise restraint. I am compelled to look for other ways to handle the situation and reluctantly switch to the second option of being understanding. In other words, I force upon myself a course of action that I had not chosen in the beginning. I wear a mask and pretend to be what I am not. Jesus cautions us against such hypocrisy. He says that the second option of trying to understand others is better; and therefore to be chosen always; and not just because the first

Chapter 17 | Empowering Professional Relationships

option is not suited to dealing with powerful people. Try to understand your customer, weak or strong, Jesus urges us. Perhaps my customer has had a bad day; perhaps he has not fully understood the context; perhaps he is begging for some appreciation; perhaps he wants to take off his mask if I will not ridicule him; perhaps he is willing to transact with me differently, if I unclench my fist.

Let us not get Jesus wrong. He does not want us to assume a passive posture. No, on the contrary, he urges us to engage in debate, disagree when our beliefs are challenged, object to the distortion of facts and firmly counter injustice. Do all of this, he pleads, as long as we do not malign or denigrate those who disagree with us. It would not be right to impute bad faith, just because of disagreements. They should not lose their dignity because they choose to oppose us; and hate should not enter our hearts.

What does understanding the customer mean? It is trying to step into his shoes; trying to look at things through his window. It is difficult because we are accustomed to looking at things through our windows. The irony is that we are ready to look through his window, only when circumstances force us into such

The Golden Rule

a compromise.

Jesus is trying to teach us to genuinely abandon retaliation; and not to use it even as a strategy. Give others the benefit of the doubt. Try not to be rash in judging others. Be respectful, rather than impudent. Value relationships, he exhorts us. Whether I transact with my wife or child or peer or banker, Jesus entreats me to look into the eyes of the person before me. Don't I see my reflection in his or her eyes? He or she is another person like me with a set of problems, Jesus explains. If only I extend a hand in friendship, that very person could surprise me by taking it.

Building happy relationships is not something that we do to others; it is something we do for ourselves. When we learn to govern our thoughts and behavior, we gain; and others gain through our changed disposition. When that happens, we are empowered. Great thinkers have told us, time and again, that when we are kind and helpful to others, we are being good to ourselves. From our own experiences, we know that it is true. Each time we performed a good deed, we were enriched.

Our understanding of Relationship Management should be different from the common perception. Let me explain myself.

Chapter 17 | Empowering Professional Relationships

Many companies direct their skill at relationship management to swing big deals with high-volume customers. Suave executives focus on these top customers who will generate big profits for them. These ambitious young people have little time or courtesy for small customers. The odd thing is that their polished veneer peels off under stress. I shall not sit in judgement. Each company should evolve strategies best suited to its needs. That is why I recommend that we evolve a strategy that suits us; a different strategy. Many companies focus on profits and strive to grab more profits. They have chosen the profit-focus-path. We too have done just that until now; with mixed results. Not any longer. I suggest that we deliberately switch to the people-focus-path. When we focus on people, they will bring us the profits we need. We too will reach the profit-destination; but by another route. No matter how good our products and how well-tested our systems, goods do not fly off shelves on their own. People must choose to buy. People must choose to distribute; and so on. People matter. Once they are satisfied, profits will follow. The people-force will drive us to achieve results that exceed our expectations. The end is important, but the means are equally important. When we look at the havoc that compromises have caused the Corporate World,

The Golden Rule

we are baffled at the short-sighted behavior of the Captains of Industry. Their obsession with profit made them myopic to the means of achieving it. The case of Goldman Sachs rocked the business world, as did the case of Satyam Computers, in India. The name of Ben Johnson, the athlete comes to mind; and more recently, Armstrong. They had a laudable goal of being the best, but they chose the wrong means and had to leave the scene in disgrace. Once again, we see that both the end and the means have to be right.

In the final analysis, we must define what we want; what our goals are. Do we want to be ranked among the top ten, the top three, in the Pharmaceutical Industry? Do we want to give our stakeholders the highest returns on their investment? Do we want to be a 'famous' company? I am not disparaging these objectives. I am only asking if they are worth the pursuit if compromises have to be made in what is important to us. They are welcome as a bonus. Have no fears. I have not become a mystic. But I try not to lose sight of our priorities. What are they? First: to be regarded as a trusted Pharmaceutical company. The Medical Profession should know that Mount Pharmaceuticals will not make a compromise on the health of patients; that our products can be

Chapter 17 | Empowering Professional Relationships

used without the slightest doubt. Second: to give customers, who buy our products, the confidence that they are getting the best, the industry can provide. Third: that those who transact with the company can count on fair dealings and do repeat business with us in trust. Fourth: that those who join us as internal customers are proud to be associated with us and view the association, not as a job, but as a career. Fifth: that we take on a role of leadership, not in chart-busting results, but in proving to Industry that value-driven performance is possible; that pursuing values is not a sign of weakness but strength. I am aware that these are long term goals. We will pursue them, even as we attempt short term objectives of successful new product launches, market penetration, entering virgin markets and so on. The main idea is to stay with the basics. What better basics can we follow than those that Jesus gave us; those that are tested over 2000 years?"

Deepak raised his hand: "May I make a point?" "Certainly, but after we take a five minute break," Victor replied.

The Golden Rule

Chapter 18
Adopting New Standards

"The real voyage of discovery consists not in seeking new landscapes, but in having new eyes."

~ Marcel Proust

After the brief break they assembled, with Deepak making the point he wished to make before the break. "Talking of basics, I was pleasantly surprised to read the interesting and far-reaching comments made by Professor Ludo Van de Heyden. Deloitte, launching its Center for Corporate Governance, put together a Panel of experts to share thoughts on Corporate Governance after the recent financial crisis. It was on that occasion that the Professor made some path-changing points: He said that stakeholders do not pay for everything; consumers do; the Public, from whom consumers are drawn, pay for everything. Logically, it is the Public interest, not that of the stakeholders, that the Company should uphold. That is why he

The Golden Rule

supports Public Capitalism in which the Company gives priority to profit of the whole society over profit of the stakeholder. The Company's primary objective should be long-term value creation and not stakeholder value addition, he maintains. That places on the Company the onus of clearly communicating its set of values to all concerned. He goes on to say that the Company should attract only stakeholders who share the same thinking and support the same professed values. If they don't agree, it is better for them to drop out. He doesn't stop there. He challenges the Company to get its employees to blow the whistle if the Company deviates from its avowed goals. To put a stamp of authority on his words, The Professor added that he and his colleagues studied 15 German Manufacturers, whose results showed that the higher the Fair Process (the name he gives to what he advocates) in Strategic Planning, the better the outcomes. The Professor was reinforcing the belief of Paul Polman, the boss of Unilever, which he declared was to work for the consumer and not the stakeholder. We recall reading Polman's words in the reading material you gave us."

Victor was impressed with Deepak's timely reference. "Those brave words warm my heart, Deepak. I draw consolation

Chapter 18 | Adopting New Standards

from the fact that we will not be called idiots, because we are now in the company of wise men." Having commended Deepak, Victor added: "We should not delude ourselves. We are not going to change the way the world transacts. We can begin by changing ourselves, to become spheres of influence. A few who transact with us will be impacted by our changed behavior and in turn, become spheres of influence in their network of relationships. It is a long process. Links in a chain will be forged. Some of our external customers will want to do repeat business with us because they have had happy transactions with us. It will be the same with internal customers. The process will widen and cover more customers – inside and outside the company - if we are consistent.

Jesus strikes us as a humble man. Even when he was rejected and assailed, he persevered in his attempts to reach out. He astounds us with the example he set before the last supper – he washes the feet of his apostles. I cannot think of any CEO who would do something similar. Jesus was from the royal household of King David; most of his apostles were fishermen. There was a huge class-divide. Yet, that did not stop him from performing the lowly act of washing their feet. He did

The Golden Rule

it to tell his apostles that service was the expression of love; that bridges not barriers had to be built; that man is enriched through humility, not impoverished. A little humility will do us no harm, especially when we try to reach out to others and are rebuffed. For example, we may try to befriend a colleague who spurns us. Building rapport with those who reject us is difficult. They need to be convinced that we are genuine; that we understand the way they feel and are ready to listen to their words and feelings. When we are rebuffed, take heart and try again; our resolve to stay on course will be tested. Service, as a mark of our love and reflection of our humility, is never easy.

Allow me to digress for a moment. How many of you have watched the movie, Gone with the Wind?" A few hands went up. "A week ago I viewed it for the second time. It is an old movie about old times; a story of romance against the backdrop of the American Civil War. Without my knowing it, I was drawn to the old world charm. I strongly recommend the movie, to those who have not seen it. Among the many things that struck me, was the contrast between the two women characters. There is Scarlett, spitting fire, manipulating people and managing situations to her advantage. In beautiful contrast

Chapter 18 | Adopting New Standards

is Melanie, her sister-in-law. She can think no evil, speak no unkind word and do no uncharitable act; even against Scarlett who feigns affection. Her life is a litany of kind words and generous deeds. Whom shall we follow: Scarlett, who scattered scorn and gathered ill will or, Melanie who sowed kindness and reaped goodwill? The answer is obvious.

Jesus spoke of choosing the narrow path, the difficult path, over the broad road. Scarlett chose the broad road to self-satisfaction; getting what she wanted. But was she happy? One wonders. Melanie chose the narrow path, finding happiness in the happiness of others; the difficult path. One could pooh-pooh this as an example drawn from the celluloid world. Fine. Let us take a real life example. Mother Teresa was celebrated for the good work she did across the world. But to those who knew her better, it was what she gave each person that mattered most. When she was interacting with a person she gave that person her everything; the need of that person got her full attention. At that time nothing else was important. As a result each transaction was enriching. People were enthralled just to have a word with her. She summed up her belief when she said: 'Love is giving the best we have'. The late

The Golden Rule

J. R. D. Tata, uncle of Ratan Tata, was known to have the same attitude. Whether he was speaking with his chauffeur or one of the top executives, in his Industrial Empire, he gave his all to the person in front of him. We know how successful he was. What am I trying to convey to you? That even in the hard-nosed commercial world there is room for understanding; there is scope for the win-win attitude. If we choose to bring to the table our all, holding back nothing, there is a fair chance that the outcome of the transaction will be better than expected. Customer or friend, the act of dealing with him in sincerity makes a difference. Jesus teaches us that.

In the extra reading material, which we distributed to you, there was a set of papers on the humanity of Jesus. In that you read of his superior intelligence, emotional intelligence and spiritual intelligence. What do we infer? When we improve our emotional and spiritual intelligence (scored as EQ and SQ), through focused effort, we too can build better relationships. Now, it is for us to tear down the walls that separate us and build bridges with those around us; starting with those in this conference room."

"You can say that again," chimed in Andy.

Chapter 18 | Adopting New Standards

Victor smiled broadly and continued: "Gentlemen and Ms Desai, I have been speaking to you from my head and my heart. Although I did prepare for this session, I must confess that at times my heart took over. Why did that happen? The answer is: Jesus' teaching touched my heart. I hope it touches yours too. Once you let him touch your heart, his words will find a way to your head. They are in my head now. Let me clarify what I just said. From my business school days I could have read in excess of one thousand books on Management and Self-Development. I am not referring to books on Science and Systems; but to those on thought-patterns. I have attended scores of seminars and read many hundred articles on such subjects. Never once have I been influenced as I was when I read The Gospels. I'll tell you why. Jesus is strikingly original – both his words and deeds. He has not copied anyone. Instead, he gave the Golden Rule body and soul. I am open to correction on what I am about to state. The books I have read, even by celebrated authors, are not original. Directly or indirectly, knowingly or unknowingly, they have employed thoughts found in The Gospels; and recycled, refashioned, extended or elaborated on those thoughts and given them labels; nice

The Golden Rule

sounding names. It is not that they plagiarized or engaged in something unlawful. No, it is just that they plucked at an idea that was already in circulation; an idea that was 2000 years old. In sharp contrast Jesus stands alone in majestic splendor, not influenced by those who went before him or his contemporaries. It is true that some thinkers, who lived before Jesus (whom Dale Carnegie refers to), gave us some lofty thoughts and important messages. But most of them speak or write like learners who painstakingly arrive at some conclusions, which they share with us. Many of those thoughts are enlightening, but don't tell the whole story. Rays from the rising sun give light, but dark shadows fall in many places. Jesus is different – he is like the sun at noon, brightening half the world at the same time. He speaks with authority; and his words have finality. He is not the hard-working learner, whom we recognize in some thinkers, but the peerless teacher, who stands apart. He understands the human predicament – the hard choices we have to make and the struggle. That is why he answers tricky questions and gives us complete messages. In short, he offers a breathtakingly refreshing new way of life. Really, he has no peers, because by example he showed how his lessons could be followed. True

Chapter 18 | Adopting New Standards

wisdom offers not just great thoughts, but great deeds as well. He lived what he taught. From what I have seen, History has not thrown up another who has been so faithful and so consistent. No wonder his words have found a way to my head. I will join the Temple Police in saying that no one has spoken like him, and the crowds who said that he did all things well.

What are Nelson Mandela's words? 'A good head and a good heart are always a powerful combination.' He should know. Let that head and heart combination work for us. Let us dare to be different in adopting people-focused policies and practices, starting with the 360 Degree Appraisal. Let it not be said of us that we feared and therefore did not attempt.

History does not lie. It does not take sides. Ten years down the line, what will the history of our company tell those who come after us: That, like our predecessors, we chose to walk the safe and beaten track, or will it record our attempts to walk the narrow-less-traveled path? Will our names be written in gold?"

He stopped, sipped some water and looked up. "I must share something more with you. Right through our discussions,

The Golden Rule

the VPs and I have had to resolve differences. Some of us believed that we had no business to drag Jesus into Corporate affairs. Some thought the idea was too radical to be practical. Jesus, a religious head, was too ancient to be a model for us today. Was he relevant? Some of you also voiced similar reservations. I am glad you did, since I would not want you to accept the idea just because I proposed it. I would want you to think about it. Reason it out. Happily, it turned out right. It turned out right, not because of our persuasive skills; far from it. At best we could take credit for begging you to read the New Testament and the other articles. Beyond that, all the persuasion you needed came from the Gospels; from the person of Jesus; from what others had to say of Jesus. It seemed so easy once you read the Gospels. Just as effectively as he handled objections from people of his time, he would have answered questions that came to your mind, as you read the Gospels. He astounded them; he had you amazed. People like Mahatma Gandhi, Swami Vivekananda and stalwarts like them were edified when they met Jesus in the Gospels. So you see you are in good company." Victor stopped and asked: "If you have any questions, I shall be happy to answer them".

Chapter 18 | Adopting New Standards

Sammy spoke for the first time: "What happens next?"

In answer, Victor said: "Mr. Chopra is trying to put some order into our various discussions. He is also doing some independent investigation. A few weeks from now, when he is ready, we shall announce the start of the 180° appraisal. In phases we shall go to 270° and 360°. That is one plan of action.

The other is to introspect. We recall the parable Jesus told of the farmer scattering seed. Seed that fell on hard ground did not take root; seed that fell on fertile ground took root and yielded a rich harvest. The parable applies to us. When our minds are prepared, we will benefit from the wisdom in the Gospels. If we refuse to condition our minds, only we will be the losers. Try to understand me. I am not suggesting anything new or radical. These ideas are 2000 years old. Sadly, we did not recognize them earlier. Peter Drucker was right when he wrote, decades ago, that doing the right thing was more important than doing things right. That nugget of wisdom cannot be ignored. He too, like others in his league, was rephrasing the wisdom of Jesus. It is time we did the right things.

As some of you know, I have read the Gospels four times.

The Golden Rule

I am looking forward to reading it for the fifth time. May I suggest that we read and re-read the Gospels and the material we have with us? I mean ponder the Gospels, as we would a book of special interest to us, and not as a religious text, and discover the wisdom in them. Then let us examine our own strengths and weaknesses. Against a checklist of points that we have from the appraisal of Jesus, let us check our own relationship building efforts. How do we compare? There is one question that we could repeatedly ask ourselves in different predicaments: **what would Jesus have done in such a situation?** An answer to that question could help us work on some of our deficiencies, so that in time, we become Professionals who handle our relationships better. In time, our seniors, peers, juniors and customers will give us a better appraisal. In time, the bottom line will look more respectable than it looks now.

Yet another plan is to re-look at all that we do. After the launch of the 180 Degree Appraisal, which will happen in a few weeks, the VPs and I will rewrite our policies to make them more people-centered. The actual rewriting will be out-sourced. One step in that direction will be the rationalizing and restructuring of the compensation-packages for the internal customers. (Jesus

Chapter 18 | Adopting New Standards

said that the laborer should receive food and a just wage). This will happen in April next year. We have started work on this big project. Even as that gets underway, we will scrutinize every single operation in the company to rid ourselves of customer-unfriendly practices, make our manufacturing processes more environment-friendly, bring in more transparency, and try to lift our dealings to a level above reproach. (Remember Jesus said that he had nothing to hide and challenged those around him to accuse him of any wrong doing. He was transparent and blameless). We will take action on a war-footing, to solve problems that stem from even minor customer-dissatisfaction. Training and retraining will get an impetus; structured to suit specific needs (recall the training Jesus gave his apostles; dealing with each, based on his need). The changes that we make will benefit both the internal and external customer. The major revamping exercise will take some time; but our efforts will be unrelenting.

I will place all our plans (old wine in new skins, to borrow a phrase from Jesus) before the Board of Directors. With the support of some like-minded gentlemen on the Board, I hope to win the Board's approval. Mr. Ravi Kumar (a majority stakeholder in the company), whom I met a few days ago, is already working on our behalf with other Board Members. We all know how powerful he is.

I can feel the winds of change blowing in my face and I like the feel. But change is not going to be easy. We will face stiff opposition inside and outside the company. Our plans will be scoffed at, our actions derided and the results we produce belittled. Changing others to our way of thinking is going to take some doing. Until then it will be a lonely walk down that narrow path. That is when our character will be on show. I hope we will not be found wanting. To combat the assault on the choices we make, we shall launch an assertive Public Relations Campaign, which hopefully will counter the propaganda against us. Besides, the PR Program will pump into the Stock Market some buoyancy.

Speaking of buoyancy, I am thrilled at the idea that our lead could lend some cheer to those who wish to learn. I had in mind other corporations and professionals, in general. I have not known of any team in the Industrial World consciously choosing to follow Jesus' Golden Rule. I have known of Christian Congregations and Groups who have tried. Some of them succeeded in part; many did not because of the compulsions

Chapter 18 | Adopting New Standards

and temptations in daily life. People outside the religious fold have not made it their driving principle. Imagine what change can come about when doctors, attorneys, judges, consultants, professors, media managers, bankers, retailers, salespersons and service providers join our ranks! How different transactions will be! When the mind-set is changed, the conversion will be easier. People need to be convinced that the Golden Rule is in their interest; that long term gains and enduring relationships can be built only through understanding and following Jesus' teachings, which are basic. Your customer, internal or external, will be good to you only if you are good to him. You can't argue against that. Unless you are fair in your dealings you cannot expect your customer to transact with you again. You can't dispute that. Once professionals like us stop to think, the logic in Jesus' words cannot be refuted. The problem is in stopping to think when we are in a mad rush to make more and more money. I am hopeful that the change will come, though slowly, when we all try. I shall be using every forum that I have – speaking and writing – to put across my conviction. Forgive me, our conviction. I urge each of you to seize every opportunity you get to spread the word. We owe it to ourselves and to Jesus. In a way, informing and persuading others in our fraternity could be part of our mission. The task is huge, but the rewards are great. While we are busy propagating the new role of the professional, we should redefine what professionalism is. Qualifications, experience, skills, commitment and competence are important. In your discussions yesterday, you agreed that a professional should optimize the use of resources. The question is: How does he do it? So the means he adopts, to optimize the use of his resources, become vital. Therefore, the picture of the professional is incomplete without the finishing stroke of the brush. Unless he can put life into his relationships – by forging lasting and fulfilling relationships – his profile is incomplete and imperfect. When he has done that he is empowered. To us, professionalism will be the achieving of our goals through empowered professional relationships; living the Golden Rule. At Mount Pharmaceuticals we shall try to perfect our profiles. With constant effort we shall try to influence others to do likewise."

Looking at his notes, Victor continued: "Some of you in the Marketing Team may harbor reservations. That will not surprise us. We will try to understand any dissenting voice, as

Chapter 18 | Adopting New Standards

long as that voice is clear and truthful. Please feel free to speak with your boss, VP Marketing. You know that my door is also open to you. It will be our endeavor to listen to your problem. We will try to marshal facts to convince you. But we may not succeed in our attempts, if your fears are deep-seated. On this account, be assured that neither your day-to-day functioning nor your career advancement will be at stake. Have no doubt. We are with you as you are with us, even if we choose to disagree on some points. But once a Policy decision is taken, as a professional please do your duty. At this point, we need to remind ourselves of the controversial statement made by Eldridge Cleaver: 'If you are not part of the solution, then you are part of the problem'. None of us wants to be part of the problem; rather, we shall be part of the solution of making Mount Pharmaceuticals a unique corporation, powered by The Golden Rule. For my part I shall lead you in this path-breaking endeavor. And that is a promise."

Pausing, Victor concluded: "Mr Samir Ghost, since I have answered your question, I take it that we can close the session. I would not want to keep you here for more than two hours. That was my promise to you yesterday."

The Golden Rule

There was prolonged applause when Victor ended his impassioned presentation. He went round shaking hands and thanking each participant for the support he received. Then he led the Vice Presidents out of the room.

The Marketing Managers and the Regional Managers were to meet for dinner at Alex's home that night. In a more relaxed atmosphere they would probably air some of their private views. Alex was ready for that.

"May I walk you down to your car?" Victor asked Alex.

"Don't bother. You look tired. Why don't you go home and get some sleep?" Alex pleaded.

"No problem. Give me the pleasure," Victor requested.

"What pleases you; should please me," Alex teased; and changing tone, continued: "You were fantastic! Absolutely fantastic! You had us enthralled, begging for more. You know something; if Christians reflected on the Gospels the way you have, the world would be a changed place. The next time I read the Gospels, it will be through your reading glasses."

"Thank you, Alex. These thoughts have taken root in me.

Chapter 18 | Adopting New Standards

I am trying to let them grow and blossom. That aside, when are you getting Antony his bicycle?"

"In a day or two," Alex said.

"What Christmas gift has Susan planned for you?" Victor probed.

"She says that it will be a surprise." Alex seemed pleased with the prospect.

"Allow me also to surprise you with a Christmas gift," Victor petitioned.

"What did you have in mind?" Alex was curious.

"Nothing very glamorous or high priced," Victor said modestly.

"I can't wait longer. Tell me," Alex entreated.

"On Monday, two weeks from the time we first met to discuss your appraisal, we shall finish it." Victor said that and looked away.

"Thank you," Alex sighed.

Victor, looking into the near future, declared: "Alex, next

The Golden Rule

year you will benefit from the 180 Degree Appraisal. Your peers will give you some bonus points."

"I will be happy to take them on board." Alex replied, smiling broadly.

References

References: Books

- The Holy Bible, The New Revised Standard Version, Catholic Edition for India. Published by Thomas Nelson for Theological, Publications in India, Bangalore (India). "The Scripture quotations contained herein are from the New Revised Standard Version Bible: Catholic Edition. Copyright (c) 1993 and 1989 by the Division of Christian Education of National Council of the Churches of Christ in the USA. Used by permission. All rights reserved".

- The Family Devotional Bible Study, India Bible Literature, Post Bag 459, Madras (India).

- Life of Christ. Fulton J Sheen, Asian Trading Corporation, Bangalore (India).

- Jesus the Teacher - Brian Grenier. St. Paul Publications, Bombay (India).

- What think you of Christ? Ian Travers-Ball, S.J. St. Paul Publication, Bombay (India).

- Responses to 101 questions about Jesus. Michael L. Cook, S.J. St. Paul Publication, Bombay (India).

- The Nazarene (Vol. I) - S.D. Arul Nathan, 4/39-1, St. Patrick Church Road, St. Thomas Mount, Madras (India).

- The Tour of the Summa of Saint Thomas Aquinas, Paul J. Glenn. Theological Publications in India, Bangalore (India).

- Essentials of Management, Harold Koontz and Heinz Weihrich. McGraw Hill International Edition.

- Leadership and the one Minute Manager, Kenneth Blanchard, Patricia Zigarmi, Drea Zigarmi. Witham Morrow & Co. Inc. New York.

- The Peter Principle, Dr. Lawrence J. Peter. Bantam Books.

- Up the Organization, Robert Townsend. Cornet Books, Hodder Fawcett Ltd., London.

- How to conduct Staff Appraisals - Nigel Hunt. How to Books Ltd., Plymouth, United Kingdom.

References

- Turned On, Roger Dow and Susan Cook, Harper Business.
- You Can Win - A step by step tool for top achievers, Shiva Khera, Macmillan India Ltd.

References: Articles

- How to run a business inspired by faith. Robert L Kinast and Judith Schloegel - (The New Leader).
- The 360° Technique - Anshun Tandon - (Business Today).
- All those in favor, Say Aye. R. Mahalaxmi - (Economic Times).
- The New People Economy. Sundeep Khanna - (Business Today).
- The right shift - Attitude is the key determinant of a successful business leader. A. Thothathri Raman- (Business India).
- How good is your EQ? Radha Dhawan - (Business

- World).

- Emotions score over Intelligence. Ashoke K. Maitra - (Economic Times).

I thank you for your time and interest in my book. I hope you liked what you read. Did the book influence you in a small way? Why not share your thoughts with other readers? Please leave a short review at Amazon.com. Thank you.

God bless you and yours.

Ignatius Fernandez